How to Share Your Faith

FRANK & ERICA KIM

How to Share Your Faith

with inspiring, real-life stories
from around the world

DPI
DISCIPLESHIP
PUBLICATIONS
INTERNATIONAL

1-888-DPI-BOOK
www.dpibooks.com

How to Share Your Faith
©1998 by Discipleship Publications International
One Merrill Street, Woburn, MA 01801

*The "Faith-Building Stories" were collected
and edited by the DPI editorial staff.*

Printed in the United States of America

Cover and interior design: Chad Crossland
Image ©1998, Photodisc, Inc.

ISBN 1-57782-069-X

*Dedicated to the brothers and sisters
of the Tokyo Church of Christ.
It is our great blessing and privilege
to watch God live among you.
Your passion to save your people
sets our hearts on fire.*

Contents

Introduction

The Heart of God • 9

Reach Out to Strangers • 13

Become a Great Friend • 29

Plant and Water in Your Neighborhood • 43

Love Your Family • 56

Be an Example on the Job • 76

Love the Poor • 91

Restore the Fallen • 109

Never Give Up • 124

Epilogue • 143

The Heart of God

The Father

The man wipes his brow with a callused hand. He sits on the porch, watching as he has done every day for years. Eyes strain to search the horizon, picking out the road trailing into a ribbon as it lazily bends out of sight. Yet, his face shows neither fatigue nor weariness. There is, rather, a curious mixture of concern, longing and anticipation. One last time his view lingers on the bluff, about to call it another day, when suddenly...a figure appears.

Immediately, he leaps to his feet. His heart races. His lips tremble. His eyes shine.

It's him. Absolutely, it's him!

Leaping down the weathered stairs, calling out to the servants, he begins to run.

The Son

It had been years, such a long time. The innumerable failures dragged at him, seemingly heavier with every step that took him home. Actually, the guilt seemed to have intensified since the day he decided to come back, for now he thought of almost nothing other than his father. The disappointment. The betrayal. How he had completely destroyed the special relationship they had shared—almost.

For somewhere deep within had remained the gnawing, inexplicable feeling that his father still waited for him, that he had not been forgotten. Often, this had annoyed him, for he had wished to close the door on his youth, wanting to escape the guilt of what he had done. Yet in the end, like a magnet reaching through the years and over the miles, that feeling is what brought him back. His father was waiting.

The bluff. The last curve. His legs become wooden; his pace slackens; he stops. Suddenly, his mouth is dry. *Suppose he's still angry? What right do I have to come back? What if he chases me away? What if he rejects me? How can he ever forgive me? But...I have nowhere else to go. I can't go back.*

His feet move forward; he rounds the bend. He looks up. The house, just as he remembered. The father, waiting, just as he had dreamed. Then...

His father rushing toward him, waving, laughing, crying—full of compassion and love. Welcome home!

The Celebration

On a cold November night many years ago, that was me. Do you remember when that was you? At a time when we knew that there was no other way, no other choice, wasn't it good to know that God had never given up? That he not only waited for us, but that he welcomed us with forgiveness, compassion and joy? As Kip McKean pulled me out of the cold baptistery waters, as I looked into the jubilant faces of the five or six friends who had come to witness a modern-day miracle (if Frank can make it, anyone can!), and as I felt the deep conviction of having been reunited with my God, I understood in that moment the greatest joy available on earth. The joy of coming home. At that same moment, what did God feel?

The heart of God. Isn't this where the Bible story begins? In the beginning, God longed for relationship and out of that desire created order out of chaos, man out of clay. Throughout the sacred pages—a history packed with adventure, heroism, betrayal, mystery and passion—the heart of God fairly pulses and throbs off the page, as time after time we are confronted by God's indomitable desire to have a relationship with man.

This true story reaches its pinnacle as God's incredible love is made manifest in the person of Jesus Christ who came to seek and to save the lost. He is the perfect reflection of how God feels about us. A shepherd who refuses to give up, a vine who will bear much fruit, an unquenchable light shining to lead lost souls out of darkness. From beginning to end, the message is vibrant with God's heart—God's passionate desire for each of us to come home.

Laser-Sharp Focus

God wants all men to be saved. We obscure the focus; we neglect its intensity; we lose ourselves in triviality. And yet, everything God has done has been directed toward that one single purpose. In Luke 15, the older son spent years with the father, but never grasped his deepest desire. Ultimately, his lack of understanding led to empty servitude and destructive bitterness: serving time, but not serving his father.

Evangelism is not about earning your way to heaven. It's not about making your name. It's not about numbers. Evangelism is nothing to be ashamed of, it's not religious, and no, it's not optional.

Evangelism is our outward reflection of having internalized the heart and the deepest desires of God. Evangelism is God's eyes roaming back and forth throughout the world, searching for those who are ready to come home. Evangelism is God's unbounded joy and heavenly celebration as the dead are raised back to life. Evangelism is clearly the heart of God.

No man or woman can claim to truly love God who does not share his most obvious and profound desire. We can and must grow consistently in our holiness, our knowledge, our humility and our love. We must daily fight the battle of emulating the character of Christ in all its perfection. But all of our spiritual growth will eventually find its fulfillment in the heart of God, the mission of Christ: to seek and to save what is lost. Without this enthusiasm, this fire burning within, all of our deeds and words threaten to become empty role-play, missing the eternal point: serving time, but certainly not serving God.

How About You?

What is evangelism to you? It is our prayer that the brief and imperfect words of this book will nonetheless be used by God to take you deeper than ever before in answering that question. For in your answer you will find a spiritual mirror in which you can see the sum of your faith. The one who loves God, loves what God loves. The one who pleases God, enjoys what God enjoys. The one who earnestly seeks God will celebrate much more than his own personal blessings from God. The true disciple's greatest ardor, greatest passion, greatest sacrifice and most unrestrained joy will be spent in the pursuit of God's greatest dream—to see his children come home. This is what sharing your faith is all about.

Reach Out to Strangers

When you were small, did your parents teach you not to speak to strangers? Did they warn you never to accept candy or other goodies from strangers? Did your mother and father tell you never to accept a ride from strangers? Most of us grew up in loving families that wanted to protect us from "those bad people."

Polar Opposites

Growing up in New York City, my father gave my brother and me code words in case we ever got kidnapped or someone other than my parents came to pick us up from school. As a further precaution, those code words changed every few months. Then one day, I became a Christian, and my Father in heaven taught me the opposite lesson.

"When the Son of Man comes in his glory, and all the angels with him, he will sit on his throne in heavenly glory. All the nations will be gathered before him, and he will separate the people one from another as a shepherd separates the sheep from the goats. He will put the sheep on his right and the goats on his left.

"Then the King will say to those on his right 'Come you who are blessed by my Father; take your inheritance, the kingdom prepared for you since the creation of the world. For I was hungry and you gave me something to eat, I was thirsty and you gave me something to drink, I was a stranger and you invited me in, I needed clothes and you clothed me, I was sick and you looked after me, I was in prison and you came to visit me.'

"Then the righteous will answer him, 'Lord, when did we see you hungry and feed you, or thirsty and give you something to drink? When did we see you a stranger and invite you in, or needing clothes and clothe you? When did we see you sick or in prison and go to visit you?'

"The King will reply, 'I tell you the truth, whatever you did for one of the least of these brothers of mine, you did for me'" (Matthew 25:31-40).

God actually wanted me to invite strangers—even into my home! What I did for the stranger, I would be doing for God.

Do not forget to entertain strangers, for by so doing some people have entertained angels without knowing it (Hebrews 13:2).

In Hebrews, it is not just a question of talking with strangers. God wants us to bring them into our homes. In this day and age of crime and murder, people do not readily trust anyone. Even kind words on a public bus attract suspicious glares from the person to whom they are addressed. As Christians, however, God wants everyone to know his word and his salvation. Unless we have the boldness to speak up to the stranger next to us, he or she may never have another opportunity to hear the gospel.

Crossing the Borders

Frank and I have been sent out on mission teams to two different countries. When we were first sent out for a training internship in the summer of 1985 to Paris, France, we had never before lived in Paris, nor did we have any acquaintances or friends there. We were complete strangers to anyone, and everyone was a stranger to us. During that summer, in three months, both Frank and I met two people each who became Christians. The experience was fun and exciting! On many nights, we had people stay over in our tiny, two-room apartment. The Lord was with us, protecting us from any unpleasant experiences. Despite my naturally suspicious nature as a native New Yorker, I learned to trust in God and make many new friends.

When we arrived in Tokyo, Japan, in 1988, we faced the same challenges as in France. Though I am Japanese, my relatives live in a totally different region of Japan, and my dialect is very different from that used in Tokyo. Making friends was much more difficult because of the language challenge. The culture was completely foreign to what Frank and I were accustomed. Once again, we were strangers in a strange and new environment.

Besides all these new challenges, most of the people we shared our faith with were atheists and had never gone to church or read the Bible even once! To them, Christianity was simply a foreign religion which had nothing to do with their lives. God, however, worked powerfully through our boldness toward strangers. Now the Tokyo church has over 1,000 people at our Sunday worship services, making it the largest weekly Christian gathering in more than several centuries of Japanese history!

Blazing the Trail

In the Tokyo church, speaking to strangers continues to comprise over seventy percent of our evangelism. We have every reason to believe that this was the primary element in the evangelism of the first-century Christians. After we have been in the kingdom for a while, we must all make determined efforts to constantly make new friends and acquaintances, because we have probably invited our other friends many times already.

The challenge to reach out to strangers is fun and exciting! It allows our faith to be raised to new levels. In fact, when we meet a new person, it is so encouraging to hear, "Yes, I would love to go with you to church this week!" Those words can uplift any Christian on any given day. Don't fall into Satan's trap and hold back. The person you meet today may be the one God has been trying to lead you to so that he or she can be saved for eternity.

Let us get rid of our worldly thinking about speaking to strangers. Listen to your Father in heaven who calls us to speak to all nations! None of them are strangers to God, because he knows and loves them all!

Faith-Building Stories

Ray Humphrey was working as an attorney and had gone to Emory University for the day to do some interviewing. Joe Cook, a disciple in the Atlanta church, had recently graduated from Emory. He had not planned to be on campus that day, but business unexpectedly took him there. As Joe walked by Ray in a campus hallway, something told him to share with him; however, he just walked on. He could not shake the feeling, so he went back and introduced himself.

Ray thought it was peculiar to be invited to church by this stranger, but he felt compelled to attend. He had accomplished a lot in his twenty-eight years, but he was unfulfilled. Ray was an outstanding high school and collegiate athlete, even competing at the professional level. He was a five-time NCAA track All-American, twelve-time Big East Champion, holder of five Georgetown University track records, seventh in the world in the long jump in 1988, alternate on the 1988 US Olympic team, and a four-time member of the US track and field team. He is a member of the Georgia, New York and Washington DC bar associations, and he was the Director of Athlete Services at the 1996 Olympic Games in Atlanta. He was definitely a busy man, but he was empty inside.

After studying the Bible for several months, Ray became a disciple. The week that Ray was baptized into Christ, he took both the Georgia and the New York bar exams and still made time to study the Bible with the brothers every day! Ray currently leads a singles ministry in the Atlanta church and also heads up the Sports Activities Program in Child Development with HOPE for Children. He has been instrumental in leading many singles to Christ.

As told by Stori Mehaffey of Dallas:

We found ourselves asking why for years. Why had we gone through two miscarriages? Why was our second daughter born four months early, weighing only one pound and five ounces and later diagnosed with autism? Why did my father pass away with cancer at the early age of forty-eight that same year? Why were we constantly moving from city to city with Kerry's jobs? Why were we the ones faced with a lifetime of caring for an autistic child? Why was my younger brother killed in a car accident when he was only twenty years old? We wanted to know why.

Kerry and I would tell each other God had his reasons for the things that happened, but we never truly believed it in our hearts. We not only had huge amounts of anger and frustration toward one another, but also toward God.

Our last move brought us to Lewisville, Texas, where I met Patty Asaad in a grocery store line. During our conversation I brought up the fact that my youngest daughter had some special needs. Some of Patty's best friends in the church also had a child with autism: Jim and Yolanda Taylor. It was amazing to see how God worked to bring us all together to help meet each others' needs. Our families quickly had a special bond.

We were asked to study the Bible the next week. I started studying and was filled with a joy I had never felt before. After my baptism into Christ, Kerry saw such radical, positive changes in me that he began studying the Bible also. He was baptized into Christ five weeks later. We both learned that God does everything for a reason. Then about a month later I had the pleasure of leading my sister Stormi to Christ.

Jay Schmidt was sitting in a cafeteria at American University in Washington DC, inviting a fellow student to his church. Gilesa McKinney overheard the conversation and invited Jay to the Washington DC Church of Christ. A graduate student in international relations at the time, Jay had grown up being very religious. He held undergraduate degrees in theology and US history, and he had been a missionary/English teacher for three years in Japan.

After attending church with Gilesa, Jay began studying the Bible with Russ Ewell. Jay's charismatic background clashed with what he began to see in the Scriptures. In his own words, "Religion teaches us what to do, not who to be. That is why, after four years of Bible college, I could know much about the Bible but be no closer to God. Religiosity does not lend itself to compassion and mercy, yet to excel in these areas is to participate in the ministry of Jesus. Jesus was merely concerned with caring about people. This is difficult to do for a Pharisee because his primary focus has always been self."

After studying for three months, Jay decided to repent, die to self, give up an exchange program in Japan and be baptized into Christ! He finished his graduate degree in DC and moved to San Francisco. The Ewells had moved there to lead the church, and Russ asked Jay to serve on the church ministry staff—where he learned more than ever how to love and serve others like Jesus did. He was later married and appointed an evangelist.

One afternoon, while knocking on doors and inviting people to a Bible discussion group on the campus of Northern Illinois University, Todd Brady and Mike Dingman came to the apartment door of Jill Bartholomay. She showed a great eagerness to attend their Bible discussion group that week and even asked if she could bring along her friend.

The following day, as Todd was working out in the campus weight room, he struck up a conversation with a guy named Phil Perez. After exchanging numbers to set up time to lift weights together, Todd walked away from Phil with the desire to build a great friendship with him and hopefully to lead him to Christ.

However, God's timing was different. As Todd stopped over at Jill's place before the Bible discussion to see if she was still attending, he was surprised to be greeted by both Jill and Phil. Not only were they dating, but they were also living together. However, before they were met by disciples, they had specifically prayed that God would send Christians and a church into their lives so they could get right with him. They knew that this was God answering their prayers.

Both Phil and Jill soon began studying the Bible, and repenting of their immorality, Phil moved out to live with some disciples. Just a month later they were married and then baptized into Christ. Currently they are on the staff of the Chicago Church of Christ.

The following is told by Curt Simmons of St. Louis:

Jesse Martin needed to pay off some of his debts so he took a second job at a local hardware store. Ed and Sandy Carr had just recently moved into a new home and needed to purchase a gas hookup for their dryer. So the Carrs went down to the local hardware store.

But more than debt reduction, Jesse needed to be saved, and more than a gas hookup for their dryer, the Carrs needed to give another person an invitation to the St. Louis Church of Christ. The Carrs were helped by Jesse at the hardware store, then began to help Jesse by inviting him to church. Jesse accepted their invitation, and two months later was baptized into Christ.

After visiting the church, Jesse began reaching out to his girlfriend who had also been reached out to separately by Sandy Carr a few days after meeting Jesse. Neither Sandy, Jesse, nor his girlfriend knew of the connection. Jesse's girlfriend began to reach out to her sister and both were soon baptized into Christ. About one year later, those sisters shared with their other sister— the three being triplets!—and she too was baptized into Christ. All three are now disciples in the Los Angeles church.

Jesse also shared his faith with his own family, and subsequently two of his sisters were also baptized. Jesse is now married (to Lora Martin) and works on the police force in St. Louis. He and his wife lead a house church in the St. Louis church and are expecting their first child.

An eleven-month tale of family fruit began at a supermarket in Franklin Lakes, New Jersey. Two single disciples, Steve Connell and Becky Witherspoon, were grocery shopping together when a woman in the store started a casual conversation with them. The friendly chat continued into a second aisle. The woman, Lisanne Knoepffler, married and a mother of two from an affluent neighborhood, found the pair quite interesting since they did not seem to be romantically involved. From the conversation, she could tell that they were simply friends.

Steve mentioned that he had recently moved back to the Hawthorne area to be closer to his church. Lisanne jumped at the chance to ask questions because she had been actively searching for a "good youth group." She was desperately trying to find a church home for her teenage daughter and son. She had grown concerned about her daughter's behavior and school relationships. Phone numbers were exchanged and the shopping trip was over. Becky followed up with a phone call and the Knoepfflers attended church the next Sunday, without their children.

At church they recognized George Egan who had invited Lisanne's husband, Jim, to come to church about four years previously. They also were impressed by George's daughter, Jenifer, and Lisanne knew she was in the right place. She noted that the racial, social and age diversity was much different than her or her husband's denominational background.

Lisanne studied the Bible and became a Christian, and her daughter, Alyssa, also was studying. Her husband Jim was attending church and participating in activities, but with much less enthusiasm. Then Alyssa was baptized into Christ, and she wrote a letter to her dad, pouring her heart out to him about her love for him and her intense desire for him to become a disciple, as well.

Three months later, Jim, an oil broker, was baptized into Christ. Then three months after that, Michael (Jim and Lisanne's teenage son) was baptized, and now they are all united in Christ!

Raised in the gang- and drug-infested city of Compton, California, LaSchaunda Kelly decided at a very young age to rebel against the stereotypes which had predetermined her future to be a "product of her environment," one of drug and alcohol abuse. An obstinate and very determined heart enabled her to persevere in her dreams of having life-changing impact in the lives of people in similar situations.

The pains and frustrations of an unyielding environment sent her in a desperate search for true security and fulfillment. However, she did not find it in her talents or wisdom, nor in the selfishly ambitious feats she set out to accomplish. She turned next to relationships with men.

A nine-month-long relationship followed, but the breakup left her utterly distraught. A daily visit to the school psychologist was the only thing which motivated her to get out of bed every day. In her despair, she cried out to God for a way out, anything that could be a source of hope.

After two months of unbearable emptiness and loneliness, she was met by a disciple and invited to church. A fearful and untrusting heart made for a rather lengthy period of Bible studies. However, the longing for God's love and the power of an indestructible life pushed her on to victory. Baptized into Christ, LaSchaunda's lifelong quest for an unfailing hope and the opportunity to have life-changing impact on others had finally ended. God answered her prayers, and she now serves God's kingdom on the staff of the San Francisco church.

Giovanna is a native of Peru. Shortly after arriving in Los Angeles, she began modeling. On her way to a modeling shoot one day, she caught a cab. As she was leaving the shoot, she noticed the cabby who had originally dropped her off was still waiting to take her home. She went over to tell him that she had not expected him to wait. The driver became insistent on taking her home. She felt threatened by the man and was not sure what to do. The streets were empty, but then she noticed a Philippine woman leaving a nearby building. Giovanna ran over to her and said, "Please pretend to be my friend and walk with me." When she felt she was out of danger, she thanked Charisse, and Charisse, being a disciple, invited her to church. A few months later Giovanna was baptized into Christ!

Story by Jeff Morris of New Hampshire:

It was about noon on a Tuesday, and I was driving home. I had a lot on my mind, and the long drive was giving me plenty of "think-time." It was about a two-hour drive back to New Hampshire, and I had picked up a bit of marijuana.

I had just spent the week with my brother, his girlfriend and her sister in Springfield, Massachusetts. I had twisted my ankle the week before so badly that my doctor gave me a note to give my boss so that I could miss work. The day after I hurt myself, my ankle was fine. I spent most of the time with the sister, whom I was sort of interested in. We played Frisbee, went bowling and climbed a local mountain. My attitude was, "Why waste a perfectly good doctor's note?"

She was the "religious" type, and I was the "druggie" type. We tried to influence each other. She would say, "You need to seek God!" Then I would tell her about all the fun she was missing. She made quite an impression on me, though, which brings us back to my drive home: The "lot" that was on my mind was seeking God.

It seemed strange to consider seeking God, since I had always professed atheism as my "religion." But I was faced with the question: "What if she's right, and I'm wrong?" So there I was, stoned, wondering how to seek God. I was ready and willing, even dead set, on seeking God, but how to do it? I had no clue. I thought, Should I buy every religious book I can find? Do I go from church to church until I find him? Should I ask people, "Where is God these days, and how can I get in touch with him?"

God must have known that I was serious because he worked quickly. I arrived at work within the next hour. I was a cook, and in the middle of the dinner rush, one of the waiters, a Muslim (who had no idea what I was thinking), came up to me, chuckling. He said, "I'm not interested in this, but maybe you are." He threw a card that a customer had just given him over the counter. It landed face-up and read, "You are invited to an informal Bible discussion group." Deep!!

Immediately after the dinner rush, I called the number on the card. I began going to the Bible discussion group on Thursday nights, and studied the Bible four times a week. About two weeks later, I was still having a tough time quitting drugs. I would sit on my bed literally with my Bible in one hand and a joint in the other, wrestling with what to do.

One night, I was in full party mode. I had expected to feel lousy in the morning, but I woke up at six, feeling great—ready to begin a new day with more energy and vision than I ever remembered having. I even cleaned my apartment! I knew in my heart that I was never going to do drugs again. No more cocaine, speed, marijuana, quaaludes or drunkenness. I cannot describe in words the freshness that I felt. It was as if God had totally removed all desire for drugs and drunkenness from me.

Less than a week later I was baptized into Christ, and I have never gone back to my old ways. There have been times when the fight for personal righteousness seemed too hard and I wanted to walk away. But remembering the way God had moved so quickly to save me eleven years ago has kept me faithful through the toughest of times. I will never leave the One who saw me the way I was and still found me worth saving!

Never underestimate the power of an invitation that you may give to the "wrong" person!

~

It is typical among young, religious Afrikaans South Africans to use their Christmas vacation to travel into "deep Africa" and work with a church for a couple of weeks, thus fulfilling their evangelistic obligation for that year. The endeavor generally ends up being frustrating and unproductive, as language barriers and ineffective Bible study do little to build conviction, let alone bring anyone to Christ.

Such was the case for Rhyno and Madelyn. When it came to sincerity and talent, they lacked nothing. But even as they traveled to Blantyre, Malawi, on an uncomfortable bus for two days, they felt the uncertainty of their lack of knowledge of the truth that they were meant to be imparting to the people they would be meeting.

That's when God intervened. Caleb and Kerrin, two disciples from Johannesburg, were on the same bus to Malawi to encourage the newly planted church in Blantyre. Over the next two and a half days (and a night spent out on the open road when the bus broke down!)—God bonded their hearts.

When they finally arrived in Blantyre, Rhyno and Madelyn could not find their party, so they stayed with the disciples for the night. They began studying the Bible with the disciples. Within the first day they realized that they actually had come to Malawi to learn the truth for themselves.

They gave up their search for the group they were meeting and joined the mission team in evangelizing and teaching the Bible. After a week they returned to Johannesburg where they were baptized into Christ and are now strong, young Christians with a dream of being on staff.

~

Kevin Murphy is a young disciple at the University of Massachusetts at Amherst. One day Kevin, who was in the library studying, started a conversation with a graduate student named John. John was interested in studying the Bible, so they exchanged numbers. A few days later Kevin called John to follow up with him and set up a time for a Bible study. John was not home, so Kevin left a message on the answering machine.

The only problem was that Kevin dialed the wrong number and left a message on the wrong answering machine, but the person who received the message was named John. John Mallon heard the message, and realizing it was meant for someone else, he decided to call the number to let Kevin know about his mistake and to tell him that he, too, was interested in studying the Bible.

The plot thickens. Kevin Murphy lives with the brother who led him to Christ, Kevin Miller. So, when John called Kevin back and told "Kevin" the story about the answering machine and dialing the wrong number and how he also was interested in studying the Bible, he was telling it to the "wrong" Kevin—Kevin Miller, not Kevin Murphy!

When these two Kevins later got together to study the Bible with John Mallon, they realized that God was not yet done amazing them. A couple in the Springfield church had been reaching out to John Mallon for the last six months. Less than four weeks after Kevin Murphy's wrongly dialed telephone call to John Mallon's answering machine, John was baptized into Christ. You are saying, "Wow! This is great!" But wait; there's more! John's wife, Sarah, was baptized into Christ one week later. Two months after John and Sarah, Sarah's daughter Meagan was baptized into Christ in the teen ministry!

At twenty minutes past eight o'clock, with no visitors arriving for the Bible discussion group, a spirit of discouragement began to descend on the group of disciples. Owen had become a Christian three months before, but since then few people had seemed interested in learning or hearing about God.

The purpose of the group was to have new friends hear the word of God, so the group fought the temptation to stay inside and "encourage" one another. Dividing into groups of two and three, they went out to meet some new people.

Dave, Carie and Owen were fighting Satanic doubts the whole time: "It seems like nobody is out tonight"; "It's already almost nine o'clock, and everything is closed"; "C'mon, we have to meet at least one new person!"

As they walked into a coffee shop, a tall, athletic-looking African-American guy in his mid-twenties was on his way out. "Excuse me, but do you play sports...?" Dave would later recall that Jeff Hickman was the only person they met that night—a night Satan thought would be his victory. Jeff, a Princeton graduate and former Tiger collegiate basketball player, had been hoping to meet some new friends in Los Angeles and get involved in sports and even a new church. He began attending the rejuvenated Bible discussion group, played on the ministry football and basketball teams and was then baptized into Christ.

Since that time Jeff has helped his mom, a coworker and his coworker's wife to become disciples. He also recently quit his near six-figure-income job with Oracle, Inc. to join the ministry staff of the arts/media/sports ministry of the Los Angeles church.

This story told by Laura Meyer, Ljubljana, Slovenia:

I was eighteen when I moved from Minnesota to Boston to get a new start, to travel and to accept a position as a nanny. I was seeking spiritual answers through New Age methods: crystals, tarot cards, psychics and anything I could get my hands on to fill me up. But nothing lasted; it was all very emotion based. I then began to sense evil when I tried to channel spirits—I realized that something was wrong. I began to pray, crying and begging God to help me find the truth. I went to several churches.

I had a friend at Boston University, and while I was at her dorm one night, a guy showed up and invited my friend to go ice skating with him after he went to church. I asked him about the church, actually trying to persuade him to let me go with him!

My first experience of the Boston Church of Christ was a "blue-jean Sunday" at the Boston Garden. I was so blown away that I found myself crying through most of the service. There were so many young people, so many races. I saw God for the first time, and I started studying the Bible that day. I was baptized into Christ about six weeks later!

I soon thought long and hard about the fact that my family and friends were lost and separated from God. I could not imagine going to heaven without them. During a quiet time, I read about the persistent widow, and I figured that if I persistently prayed for my family and friends, they would eventually be saved. So I started praying every day, sometimes twice a day, for them.

About four months later, Brenda, one of my sisters, moved to Boston to start a nanny job. I was so excited! At first Brenda was very negative about the church and refused to come to anything. Finally, she said that if I went to aerobics with her, she'd come to a Bible discussion group with me. She came, loved it, started studying the Bible and was baptized into Christ shortly thereafter. God has used her powerfully to bring many women to Christ, and she is now engaged to be married to an incredible man of God! They are now on the ministry staff of the Boston church, and I am currently on the mission field in Ljubljana, Slovenia.

Rico van Rooij, a Dutchman, wondered which way to go in life. He studied business, joined the army and worked many jobs in his home country. He enjoyed his hobbies: sports, helping handicapped people, motor driving, partying and reading books. But he felt restless, so he went on a trip around the world. In Auckland, New Zealand, he listened to a gospel choir performing on the street. He went to their church service and "prayed Jesus into his heart." Rico bought a Bible and read through it as he continued his travels.

Wondering about many faith issues, he arrived in Australia, where Jonathan Whiting and Anton King invited him to the Sydney Church of Christ. Rico learned that there is more to a relationship with God than accepting Jesus into your heart. He wondered why they spent so much time teaching him, a foreigner. For the first time in his life he saw the unconditional love of God in these awesome "Aussie" disciples.

Rico was then baptized into Christ, and as a young disciple, he invited a German couple, Christian and Sabine Herbst, who would later become disciples and lead the Munich church. Moving on to London, he met eight people in one year who eventually were baptized! Then God fulfilled his dream of going back to Holland in 1991 on the mission team to Amsterdam. He has met and led many to Christ there, most of whom are still strong disciples. Others became leaders in the church in their home countries, like Ranny de Vries in Suriname and Vincent Semeleer in Curaçao.

Rico now works for a bank, is a songleader and sometimes preaches on Sunday. Together with Isabelle Otten, a great sister who works as a doctor, he feels privileged to lead the ministry to working singles in Amsterdam. Most of all, he is grateful to God for saving him and showing him which way to go.

Become a Great Friend

Best friends. Buddies. Companions. Partners. Is friendship important to you? Do you enjoy making new friends? Are your friends an essential part of your life? What do friendships mean to you? Jesus calls us his friends:

> "You are my friends if you do what I command. I no longer call you servants, because a servant does not know his master's business. Instead, I have called you friends, for everything that I learned from my Father I have made known to you. You did not choose me, but I chose you and appointed you to go and bear fruit—fruit that will last. Then the Father will give you whatever you ask in my name" (John 15:14-16).

Though we are servants to Jesus and to God, Jesus sees us as partners and companions...friends. Everything that Jesus learned from the Father, he has shared with us, his friends. As friends, we share the same purpose as the Master. Ultimately, it is through our relationship with the Lord and consequently, with our friends, relatives and neighbors that we are assured of abundant fruit in our lives. Let us take time to examine our friendships which are essential in bearing much fruit.

Friendship Defined

In the following passages, Jesus gives us two major keys to evangelizing the world. Both describe the same heart and mind-set necessary to guide others to God's eternal home, heaven. (Of course, this concept is based on the premise that we each first have a deep and special relationship with the Lord!)

> "My command is this: Love each other as I have loved you. Greater love has no one than this, that he lay down his life for his friends" (John 15:12-13).

> Jesus replied, "The hour has come for the Son of Man to be glorified. I tell you the truth, unless a kernel of wheat falls to the ground and dies, it remains only a single seed. But if it dies, it produces many seeds" (John 12:23-24).

Jesus set the standard by dying for us. He redefined love in a spiritual and eternal way. This same kind of love must result from our own personal association with God. Then and only then will we be able to build the kind of relationships that will affect others for Christ. Let us imitate our Lord, because there are no short cuts or easy methods for saving souls. We need to be willing to even give our lives for the salvation of others. This is true spiritual friendship.

Painful Truth

I remember the beginning of the arts/media ministry in Tokyo. We had a brother who played the keyboard and two sisters, one of whom was an actress. I even got a job in two movies and did some modeling as well. However, in the first two months, we had no fruit. We were very discouraged at that time. We got together, and Frank asked us all to write down two or three positive words to describe our group. People wrote: hard-working, lots of potential, eager, fun, talented, evangelistic, etc. Frank then opened his Bible and began reading 1 Corinthians 12:31-13:1-3, 8 (emphasis added):

> And now I will show you the most excellent way.
> If I speak in the tongues of men and of angels, but have not love, I am only a resounding gong or a clanging cymbal. If I have the gift of prophecy and can fathom all mysteries and all knowledge, and if I have a faith that can move mountains, but have not love, *I am nothing*. If I give all I possess to the poor and surrender my body to the flames, but have not love, *I gain nothing....Love never fails.*

My heart felt pangs of embarrassment and guilt as I heard the words of this scripture. I suddenly understood why we had no fruit in this ministry. Frank preached a simple message. As he spoke, I became more and more convicted of my lack of love. He spoke about how all the words we had used to describe our group were accurate. We were even very evangelistic! God had given us all the tools, yet no one had written love as the outstanding quality of our group. Yet, love was the most needed and significant aspect, because our love reveals God to others.

With tears in our eyes, all of us decided to repent of our worldly and humanistic efforts. As a result, God worked powerfully over the next few months. Many people were baptized because of God's love evidenced in us—not because of the brothers' and sisters' talents and abilities! Now, three years later, the arts/media ministry is one of the fastest growing ministries in the Tokyo church! To God be the glory!

Heart Check

So often the people that we reach out to become "projects" rather than best friends. We were never "a project" to Jesus when he died on the cross for us. It was Jesus' love and his desire to have a relationship with us that enabled him to give his life for us. When we love deeply like Jesus did and build deep friendships with our non-Christian friends, they will see Christ in us.

This "project mentality" often robs us of the joy of making friends while sharing our faith. No one comes to a faith in Jesus without a Christian's genuine love, sacrifice and tears.

During my ten years in Tokyo, there has only been one year that I have not been able to meet someone who became a disciple. That year, I was seriously ill with lupus. I also struggled spiritually. In the end, I learned patience in every area of my life, as well as a trust in God about my personal effectiveness. My various friendships grew deeper because I appreciated the short life that God had given me.

Since that time, so many of the people that I have shared my faith with and with whom I have studied have become friends that I love in an inexpressible way. When they struggle, I am driven to my knees. When they are not happy, I yearn to see their smiles again. When they rejoice, I celebrate with them. Last year, my very special friend Satoko became a Christian. Before Satoko would study the Bible with me, we developed a deep friendship over a period of five months. Though it took nearly a year before she was baptized into Christ, I have been blessed with a friendship that will last not only a lifetime but into eternity!

Bushels of Fruit

There is no easy method or technique to helping our friends to know Christ. It is truly the result of being like Christ and becoming best friends with them through Christ's love. Through that attitude and heart of sacrifice, God will fill our branches with much fruit. Accordingly, we will glorify the Lord and carry out God's plan to bring the gospel to every corner of this world.

As you read the next few pages of this book, I pray that you are transformed not only in knowledge but in motivation as you deepen your desire to seek and to save the lost. May this chapter serve you by teaching you how to become a better friend. And in due course, may you glorify our God with abundant fruit!

Faith-Building Stories

Story told by Jeff Chacon of Orlando:

I met him in my Spanish class in college while living in San Diego. He was fit and handsome and to call him a serious person would be an understatement. This guy was intense! The first time I invited him to a Bible study on campus, he said, "No, thank you," and that was it. I didn't talk to him again for a while. I just figured he was not open.

But then one day I saw him at a political rally on campus. I discovered that he was the president of a Mexican-American political organization on campus. I thought, "Wow, what an impact this guy could have in the church," and I decided to invite him again. I don't remember how many times I invited Robert to come to Bible study before he actually came. Somehow I knew that Robert was open, and I was determined to win him over to Christ.

Robert drove a "low-rider." In the early '80s in San Diego, that was cool. I knew that if I was going to help Robert to become a disciple, I would have to become part of his world, so I began to take an interest in the things he was into. Soon I was thumbing through low-rider magazines, going with him to Chicano Park to volunteer for the Cinco de Mayo party, sharing my life and faith all along the way.

I will always treasure the times when we would study the Bible together—sometimes we laughed, sometimes we cried, and often we disagreed sharply, but always we were building an incredible spiritual friendship. Then one day Robert was finally ready to make Jesus Lord and be baptized as a disciple.

Today Robert Carrillo is an evangelist in the kingdom of God. He has served on the mission field in Mexico City and has led the churches in Puerto Rico and Miami. He now is a region leader in the New York City church with his awesome wife, Michele. And we will always be the very best of friends.

Story told by Kenny Hester of Boston:

I was working as night-shift security officer in downtown Boston. One night I noticed a young lady seated on the bench near the security desk. I later found out that she was also working as a security officer. I invited her to church, asking her if she believed in God. She said she wanted to come to church and that she was interested in knowing more.

She then called me to tell me that she could not make it that first week. I was impressed because very few people initiate the phone call to let you know that they cannot come to a worship service. The second week was the same. By the third week I figured she just was not open.

I had another friend who had been studying the Bible and who, for no apparent reason, had stopped studying. Then about two weeks later, I saw the woman whom I had invited previously taking a break at work. I sat down with her, and we talked more about her coming to church. In the middle of the conversation, the guy I had been studying with before walked in and gave the woman a kiss! At that point I understood why he had stopped studying. I also realized that if she were to become a Christian, he had to become one first.

Starting on the day that I saw him kiss her, I opted to use my hour-and-a-half break at work to pray. I would go up to a vacant room, get down on my knees and pray to God. One morning I went down to the lobby after praying and had a talk with the guy. I asked him when he was going to start studying again, and he said that he didn't know. So I asked him what he thought would happen if he walked outside, was hit by a car and died: "Would you be with God or not?" He hesitated for a minute, said he would not be with God and then turned and walked outside. When he came back in, he was in tears and said he wanted to get right with God. We studied the Bible every day, and one week later my friend was baptized into Christ!

As my new brother in the Lord began to grow spiritually, his relationship with our woman friend began to change. Soon she came to church and was baptized into Christ.

Interestingly enough, Marverly, the woman in this story, is now my wife of four years. God has blessed us with a beautiful daughter, and together we strive every day to give glory to God.

Katherine Sapp, daughter of Steve and Kim Sapp, leaders of the Atlanta church, was a cheerleader and was very caught up in being popular at school. Her parents prayed desperately for years that Katherine would become a disciple. Katherine was rude to other disciples at her school, not wanting to be seen walking or talking with them because they were not "cool." She did not care who she hurt as long as she was popular at school with her friends.

Julie Notebloom, a teen ministry leader, persevered for three years as Katherine's friend, gaining her trust and respect. Eventually, Katherine saw her life becoming empty like the girls on her cheerleading squad and realized that she did not want that for her life. While attending the summer church camp, Katherine expressed this to Julie and to the other disciples. As she studied the Bible, she realized how much she had hurt her family, her friends and, most of all, God. She was radical in repenting of her worldliness and decided not to try out for cheerleading the next year because the temptations would be too great. She was baptized into Christ at the end of the summer.

Through the prayers and perseverance of her family and Julie, Katherine is now a powerful, fired-up disciple at her high school.

This story told by Shade O'Quinn of Dallas, Texas:

I grew up the only child of a prominent Protestant minister. My mother and father were very loving and giving parents. My father was my hero.

During college I became friends with a classmate named Charles. I was impressed by Charles' knowledge of the Bible and his evangelism and was finally persuaded to visit his church. The week that Charles and I sat down to study the Bible together was not only finals week at school, but also the week before I was to get married to Sally, my fiancée.

After only three days of studying the Bible with my friend, I was resolved to be baptized into Christ as a disciple. I knew that the faith I had come to accept was radically different than my father's and that my decision would change everything in our relationship. I remember calling my dad and my fiancée before I was baptized and explaining my decision to put God first.

After a long time in prayer, I went home and married Sally that weekend. By the grace of God, Sally was eventually baptized into Christ as a disciple.

Shortly after I was baptized, my father disowned me. Although this hurt, I kept on pursuing a relationship with him. Over the years we were able to share openly about our differences, and our relationship became more honest. My father was still my hero, but not my god. Ten years later, my father passed away. Although it hurt to lose him again, I was at peace with him and with my heavenly Father.

Told by Curtis Gressett of Dallas:

Kristina and I divorced after only two years of marriage due to our selfish natures, hard hearts and chemical addictions. We stayed in touch and became good friends over the next six years. We each got involved in other relationships, but none of them lasted.

Four years later, we started a relationship again, but the yelling and arguing returned and escalated to intolerable levels. We split up six months later. During this time Kristina called an old coworker who recently had become a disciple and who invited her to the Phoenix Valley church. Kristina began studying the Bible and was baptized into Christ the next month. She started reaching out to me, but I did not see my need for God.

Then my aunt called to inform me that my mom was dying. I went to see her for a few days, and then she died. The devastation I felt helped me to see my need for God. Kristina introduced me to several disciples, and they studied the Bible with me. I changed my life for God and was baptized into Christ.

Kristina and I began to be interested in each other again. We now could appreciate each other as individuals and learned how to love as Jesus intended, not as the world intended. My company relocated me to Dallas in May, and with much prayer and advice, Kristina and I joyfully remarried!

We became a part of the chemical recovery ministry in the Dallas/Fort Worth church, and since graduating from this ministry, we have learned to deal with the substance abuse and the hidden feelings that wrecked our first marriage. We are grateful to God for bringing us back together and for his many blessings he continues to bestow upon us, including renewing my relationship with my daughter Jennifer (from a previous marriage) whom I had not seen in nine years.

As told by Michiel Middendorf of Amsterdam:

Rosa and I had started living together in Madrid, Spain, both coming out of broken relationships. I was successful by worldly standards, managing a TGIFridays restaurant, making good money and having many "friends." However, never was I able to maintain a true loving relationship with anybody, including my ex-wife. Immorality, unfaithfulness and selfishness (putting my career above all) ruined my marriage.

I had never looked to God. The religious world had convinced me to go only one way: atheism! Then Rosa and I were invited to a party thrown by some disciples. A party with Christians? What do we wear? Will they have beer? What kind of music will they play? Little did I know that that night, for the first time in my life I was going to meet sincere, honest and loving people. I could not deny what I experienced. I was impressed by the friendship that Roy Larson and David Seavey were building with me. I had one problem, though: I did not believe in God.

Growing up in a denominational church, I did not know anything about the Bible. When Rosa started studying the Bible and David asked if I was interested, I agreed to study out of curiosity and thought, Why not? If these people's lives come out of what they believe in, at least it will be interesting.

The first time we opened the Bible was in a bar in downtown Madrid and I thought, These guys are cool. They are super-relatable. A little later, we made a Bible study plan. After six days, I thought I could decide to follow Jesus. But then the difficulties came....

Rosa was about to leave Spain to visit her mother in Peru for several months. There was no church in Peru yet, so Roy advised her not to travel right away in order to grow spiritually first. Family is the top priority for most Latin cultures, so Rosa was very reluctant to seek the kingdom first. I realized at the same moment I was not able to make Jesus my Lord, either. My fear was that I would lose Rosa by becoming a Christian. I realized that I completely depended on her. I also thought that she should go to Peru instead of being concerned with her spiritual life. I realized I wasn't ready to make my decision.

I was scheduled to leave for the US for my work within three days, so Roy simply encouraged me to continue to study the Bible over there. God had different plans!

The next day at church, it all became clear to me. God was asking me for the one thing I wasn't willing to give up: Rosa. After the service, I cried. Right then and there I made my decision to get baptized into Christ, no matter what Rosa was going to do.

I shared my decision with the brothers, and then as I told Rosa, she cried and we hugged. At the same moment that I had,

Rosa had made her decision to get baptized. She wanted to follow Jesus and postpone her trip to Peru until she would be strong enough spiritually.

God was just waiting for me to get my priorities right, and when I did put him first, he blessed me right away! He also let Rosa and me grow closer to him, apart from each other. I traveled throughout the US on business as a young disciple; I saw and learned a lot in different churches. Rosa went to Peru later for a couple of months and came back to Madrid. After eight months, I returned to Madrid to open and manage the Hard Rock Café there, and Rosa and I continued dating. Then months after that, God blessed our patience with a dream wedding and a dream marriage. We are now leading the Amsterdam church in the Netherlands, my home country.

Recently, Rosa's mother was baptized into Christ at a European Missions Conference in Paris, and she then baptized her mother into Christ in Peru at age ninety! Rosa and I have also been blessed this year with a beautiful baby girl.

Don and Debbie St. Claire were met by Jennifer Salberg, leader of the arts, media and professionals women's ministry in the Atlanta church. Jennifer was walking with her daughter Hannah in Lennox park. Don and Debbie were there with their two young children, and Jennifer struck up a conversation with them. She discovered that they were both doctors: he a cardiologist and she an internist. As it turned out, Don was just finishing his residency at Emory, and they were going to be leaving for California where he had secured a teaching position at Stanford University. They were both interested in coming to church, although he expressed little belief in God, and she was Catholic.

Debbie came to a worship service first, loved it and agreed to study the Bible beginning that week. Don was not as eager, but was very open to friendship. Very quickly he and Debbie and Jennifer and her husband, Larry, became best friends. Debbie was studying consistently, and after a short time Don began reading the Bible with Larry. Don's faith began to grow.

After six weeks Debbie was ready to be baptized into Christ, and Don was getting closer. They had to decide whether they would stop studying in Atlanta and begin again with the church in California, or give up the position Don had at Stanford and stay in Atlanta with no guaranteed medical positions for them. They made the decision to do what would be best for them spiritually and give up the job in California. The next day Don went to the head of his department at Emory to see if there might be a position available there. This is simply unheard of in the medical field, but for a disciple it was a question prompted purely by faith. He was offered a job two days later at Emory and was baptized into Christ ten days later, one week after his wife!

As told by Robert Cooper:

Before the World Wide Web became globally popular, I was a subscriber to Prodigy, an Internet provider. They sent bumper stickers to their members so that they could identify each other. I decided to put it on my car and put my member ID number on it, which was encouraged.

On my daily commute, I took back streets most of the way because I did not want to drive with the sun in my eyes on the highway. A disciple in the LA church was also a Prodigy member, and our driving route to work was similar only for a few blocks. One morning she was close enough to my car to notice my bumper sticker and the ID number on it. She noted the number and contacted me immediately via electronic mail.

She and I built a friendship via e-mail. She was shrewd enough not to get religious in our e-mails (which was good because I don't think I would have continued to build a friendship). After a few weeks, we exchanged phone numbers, and she invited me to a party.

At the party I was impressed by the diversity of the people there. I felt that under the surface, Los Angeles was very racially divided. Later, of course, I found out that the people at the party were disciples. But I didn't come to church immediately. It took six months of God humbling me before I turned to him for help. I went to church, started studying the Bible and was baptized into Christ a few weeks later!

As told by Wyndham Shaw of Boston, Massachusetts:

Adam Jenkins is the fourteen-year-old, high-school friend of our son, Sam. They have gone to school together since the second grade. Adam is a straight 'A' student and excels on both his football and basketball teams. Sam had brought Adam to numerous teen ministry events and to several church services over the years. Adam also came to Sam's baptism and has since told us that he had decided at that time two years ago that he would one day do the same!

Last September God worked in Adam's life through an emotionally down day when he stayed home from school. After some intense soul searching he told Sam how he was feeling, and Sam told him he needed God in his life and asked him to study the Bible.

Just before his baptism Adam began to approach his father, Steve, about coming to church with him. One Saturday afternoon he asked him to come the next day, and Steve made the excuse of needing to clean out the pool and being too busy. Steve then went into the house and started to tell his wife, Linda, about his conversation with Adam when it hit him. Steve, who is the assistant superintendent of the Somerville, Massachusetts, school system, discussed with Linda the irony of being a parent whose teenage son was asking him not if he could do drugs, get drunk or stay out all night but if his dad would go to church with him. He knew that he was wrong and went back to Adam to say he would go. Steve and Adam have been coming ever since!

Steve and Linda were baptized into Christ, following Adam's example, after they both studied the Bible and wrestled through their individual issues.

I remember Steve beginning to study "only to check out what his son was getting into." During the second study he noted that maybe he could learn some things about God, as well. He was having a hard time coming to grips with who is lost and saved and remembers the pivotal night when he almost decided to stop studying because of the emotional implications of the truth. I had made the point that if he would not obey God's standard, he might as well throw the Bible out and make himself God. After several sleepless nights and much consideration, Steve decided to let God be God and was baptized into Christ.

Linda continued to study the Bible and now the whole family, except for six-year-old Mark, have been baptized into Christ—and he wants to know when he can do it! Also, both of Adam's grandmothers have been visiting the church and one of Steve's high-school football buddies is now studying the Bible with him! Truly it is exciting to see teens lead their friends to Christ and then teens leading their families to Christ. To God be the glory!

Plant and Water in Your Neighborhood

On one occasion an expert in the law stood up to test Jesus. "Teacher," he asked, "what must I do to inherit eternal life?"

"What is written in the Law?" he replied. "How do you read it?"

He answered: " 'Love the Lord your God with all your heart and with all your soul and with all your strength and with all your mind'; and, 'Love your neighbor as yourself.' "

"You have answered correctly," Jesus replied. "Do this and you will live."

But he wanted to justify himself, so he asked Jesus, "And who is my neighbor?"

Luke 10:25-29

The teacher of the law wanted to know how he could attain eternal life. When Jesus gave his answer—to love God and to love his neighbor as himself—this "religious" man wanted to justify himself. He desired to know exactly who his neighbor was. It seems he did not want to love anyone he did have to love. Notice that he did not make excuses regarding his personal relationship with God. He assumed that he loved God according to the Law, separating in his mind his relationship with God from his love for his neighbors. In the same way, we often find ways to justify not reaching out to our neighbors, while thinking that our relationship with God is exemplary.

Jesus loves our neighbors. Whether we know them or not, each of them is special to our Father in heaven. Though we need to love all of our neighbors (i.e. the people with whom we come in contact each day), we cannot forget, in particular, those who live right in our own neighborhoods. We have no excuse for not reaching out to the people who live so close to us. Let us not become like the teacher of the law who excelled in making excuses.

Love in Any Language

In these modern times, the neighborhood is no longer a close-knit community of friends on whom we rely, as in past generations. Moreover, most people do not even know who lives next door or two doors down from them! As Christians, however, we can take the initiative to build ties with the people who live in our immediate vicinity. There is a reason why they live near us!

> "From one man he made every nation of men, that they should inhabit the whole earth; and he determined the times set for them and the exact places where they should live. God did this so that men would seek him and perhaps reach out for him and find him, though he is not far from each one of us" (Acts 17:26-27).

The reason that a certain family or a certain person lives next door to us is so that they will have a chance to respond to God's message. Does your neighbor even know that you are a Christian? Do they see the difference between you and all their other neighbors?

Since we moved to Tokyo, God has blessed Frank and me with the opportunity to share the gospel with many Japanese nationals. Initially, there were many challenges, especially because Frank did not speak a word of Japanese (his family background is Korean). Despite this obvious handicap, Frank was determined to learn the language and to help the people in Japan to be evangelized for Christ.

Where did we start evangelizing all of Japan? We started in our own neighborhood. When we were trying to decide where to live, God guided us to a wonderful neighborhood where we eventually resided for eight years. At the end of that time, over thirty Christians lived in our immediate vicinity! Many were converted there, and others had moved into the area to be closer to some of the other disciples.

I recall the first neighbors that were converted, just months after we arrived. They lived right down the street from us. I was eight months pregnant with my second child, and upon the orders of my doctor, Frank and I took a daily walk to the park. When we arrived at the park one day, we met a young woman with her newborn baby. We were immediately drawn to each other, since I looked ready to burst with my pregnancy, and she had a tiny baby. The three of us talked and exchanged phone numbers. Her name was Keiko Masuda, and she was actually excited to know that Frank was a minister!

The next day, Keiko called me and invited me over for tea at her home. Since I was not yet completely fluent in Japanese, I fervently prayed for God to guide our conversation and to help me speak God's word powerfully. During our few hours together, she shared about her marriage problems, her struggles with raising her children and the emotional turmoil inside her heart. I shared a few scriptures and was able to talk about how Jesus had changed my life. I went home so excited that day.

A few days later, Frank and I decided to have the Masudas over for dinner. We fixed up our living room as best we could and prepared a candlelight dinner. I translated for Frank that evening, as he shared about our marriage and how much we love each other. They were astounded to hear a couple actually share such intimate feelings about each other to a third party. In Japan, by custom, people do not share such personal emotions with any outsiders. Yet, Keiko and her husband, Yasushi, were touched by the sharing and were eager to come to church to find the answers that would help them with their marriage and with raising their children.

I appreciated my husband so much that evening! Though he spoke no Japanese, he did not hold back from sharing his faith. He made sure that Yasushi and Keiko could see Jesus in our lives, even with me translating! They felt Frank's heart and commitment through his eagerness to communicate God's love. Love in any language comes straight from the heart!

Straight from the Heart

Meeting our neighbors is often easy, but the greater challenge may lie in the steps that follow. The friendship and the kind of relationship we build can often determine whether someone will come to church with us or not. Our relationship with the Masudas allowed us to have great talks with them, but it took many weeks of continual contact before they actually attended a church service. In the meantime, I made a point of sharing scriptures with Keiko whenever it was appropriate. The reason that they were not able to come to church very consistently was that Yasushi had an extremely demanding job that required him to work on many Sundays.

We were often bewildered in deciding what approach to take to help a busy businessman and his wife. Since Yasushi would leave extremely early in the morning and arrive from work very late at night (most of the time between 9:00 pm and 1:00 am!), Keiko would often keep the children awake until almost midnight so that they could spend time with their father. Faced with a schedule this challenging, we prayed daily for guidance and opportunities from God. We also relied on other Christians to help us reach out to Yasushi and Keiko.

> Trust in the Lord with all your heart
>   and lean not on your own understanding;
> in all your ways acknowledge him,
>   and he will make your paths straight (Proverbs 3:5-6).

Ultimately, since Keiko had a lot more time available than her husband did, she was baptized into Christ within a couple of months. Though Yasushi was eager to study the Bible, his job schedule would not allow him to do so. Amazing as it may sound, Keiko tape-recorded all of our Bible studies together. When Yasushi arrived home at night, he would first help bathe his children (even at midnight!), and then he would sit down with Keiko and listen to the tapes of our Bible studies.

Several weeks after Keiko was baptized into Christ, Yasushi had still not been able to study directly with Frank. By faith, Frank challenged him to use his summer vacation from work to study the Bible every day. Yasushi agreed to the request and canceled a planned family trip to his hometown. Yasushi had been an atheist, but daily Bible studies during that single week resulted in God's miracle. One dilemma was that Frank had to have all the studies translated by a Japanese brother, so it took twice the usual amount of time. Despite all the obstacles, God triumphed, and Yasushi was baptized into Christ that next Sunday!

Sometimes we are afraid to take that step of faith to help someone to be saved. There will be times when we have to lay out the challenges in order for someone to see their need to study the Bible. We need to trust God to lead us in the right direction when we lead others to make tough decisions. I believe that it was Frank and other brothers' patient love for Yasushi that allowed him to finally make a radical decision of faith to study the Bible.

Love Pulls Us All Together

God promises that sacrifices made in faith will surely be rewarded (Hebrews 11:6). Yasushi and Keiko have continued to give their best to God, resulting in tremendous growth in their spiritual lives and in their family. They have helped to develop the children's ministry in Japan and serve as deacons in the Tokyo Church of Christ. Our friendship with them is genuine and profound. Their two oldest children are the same age as ours, so we have been able to reach out to and study with many neighbors and families from their school together. Our friendship with the Masudas has and continues to have an eternal impact. Even those neighbors who have not become Christians (yet!) have deeper relationships with one another. It is definitely God's love that pulls us all together.

Let's take the time to look at our neighborhoods and see the potential that they have for God's kingdom. It is a mission field that God has given us in which to plant and water. Some of the results will come quickly. Others will come after many years. For most of us, we will live in our neighborhood for several years—maybe for most of our lives. We need to have a renewed attitude of faith toward our neighbors: God put them there for a reason. Let us make a decision today to love with the same love that Jesus has for us. Love your neighbor as yourself, and in time, the planting and watering will result in fruit that will last into eternity!

Faith-Building Stories

Victor Romero became a Christian while he was a student at the University of Texas at Arlington. He was pursuing a degree in music and played the drums with a local band that performed around the Dallas area. He was excited about his new purpose and began to share his faith with all his friends. Then he found out he had cancer. This led to a series of surgeries and chemotherapy to control and cure the disease; but no lasting progress was made. Finally, the doctors sent Victor home with the idea that nothing could be done, except to make his last days as comfortable as possible, which they thought would be few.

Victor's neighbor was a young man named Mike Kopf. Victor shared his faith with Mike and tried to reach out to his friend. However, Mike was not interested. The doctors and Victor's friends were amazed at Victor's spirit and will to live. He kept on defying the predictions of his physicians: first by a month, then two, then six and then a year. Victor just kept hanging on to life!

All the while he was still reaching out to Mike, his friend. The disciples would come and have communion and read and study the Bible with Victor, for he was too weak to get out of bed. Eventually, Mike began reading the Bible to Victor. Mike continued to see the love of the disciples for one another, and then he began to study the Bible. He came to church, and Victor was energized by the thought of his friend becoming a Christian. Mike and the brothers would make special arrangements to have a stretcher for Victor that allowed him to participate in the worship services.

Then on Easter Sunday Victor Romero took the confession of his friend, Mike Kopf, and rolled over on his stretcher to place his hand on his friend while he was baptized into Christ.

A few months later Victor went home to glory. Mike is a leader in the Dallas church now. What kept Victor going? Like Paul, he still had fruitful labor to accomplish.

As told by Robert Carrillo, who now lives in New Jersey.

I remember sitting in my car in San Juan, Puerto Rico, at about 8:30 pm, thinking about the events of the day. I thought I would take time for a prayer before going in the house. I had been out sharing my faith without much success and was praying that God would soon lead me to someone open to the gospel. From the time of our arrival in Puerto Rico, my wife and I had prayed daily to bring a couple to Christ who would become great friends and help us to evangelize the island. As I sat there in our driveway, it occurred to me that it probably was not the safest place to be. I had been warned about the high crime rate in San Juan, including the all-too-frequent car jackings and killings.

Right then I saw in my rearview mirror several shadows quickly pass by. My first thought (or hope) was that maybe some fellow disciples were sneaking up to scare me. I got out of my car quickly to see who it was. They were not brothers! Four young, masked men demanded I give them my car keys at gunpoint—I quickly obeyed. While all this was going on, I heard screams coming from a porch a few houses down the block.

The car jackers jumped into my car and sped off. Then a black Mustang came roaring up, and the driver asked me if I wanted to go chase them down. As it turned out, he was my neighbor whose wife had been screaming. He was ready to go after them to get my car back! All I could think was, "God answered our prayer!" I knew he and his wife would become Christians.

William Torruella was a professional tennis instructor and Aixa an artist, and both had noble hearts searching for God. A few weeks later, after studying the Bible, they were baptized into Christ. A few months later, Aixa's sister and then her mother both became Christians. Then William's parents, his sister and brother-in-law and a cousin were all baptized.

William and Aixa now have new careers: They are on the ministry staff, leading the great Puerto Rico church.

Melanie Berry is a professional woman from New Jersey who had been invited to church by a neighbor, Lorraine Langevine, for two years. Lorraine is a disciple with two teen daughters, Beverly and Rebecca, also disciples, and a son, Michael. Melanie visited the church sporadically, and even started studying the Bible, but did not see her need for God for over a year. However, she began to have difficulties with her teen son. She observed the differences between her children and Lorraine's children who were disciples and very actively involved in the teen ministry.

Melanie decided to start coming to church again regularly, studied the Bible and became a disciple. Very shortly after that, her teen son, Jordan, became a disciple, and then her daughter, Morgan, was baptized into Christ. Her son has since then led two friends and one of their mothers to Christ.

As told by Mike Hodges of Orlando:

As a young disciple, I eagerly desired to be effective in my evangelism, but I was plagued with fear and cowardice. One day I came home after a long day at work and decided that I would go out for a run. I wavered between taking some church invitations or not. I thought about it for several minutes and then got indignant that I had decided in my heart that sharing my faith was optional. I immediately got down on my knees and poured out my heart to God. As I prayed, I found myself demanding that God put someone in my path on my run who would become a disciple. I felt somewhat disrespectful being so demanding, but I knew deep in my heart that he would bless this kind of faith and attitude. I struck up a conversation with a man running in the same direction and I shared my faith with him, but he was not really interested.

I felt like I was on the brink of discouragement. I began to pray fervently for God to give me another opportunity to share with someone who would be open. I prayed that God would put a couple we had passed previously in my path. As I saw them approaching, fear seized me and part of me said, "Don't embarrass yourself; they won't be interested." I ran past them a few yards until another part of me said, "You just prayed about this! How can you not share with them?!"

I turned around, pulling a slightly sweaty church invitation out of my pocket, and shared with them how great my church was and how much I wanted them to come. The woman said, "We were just talking about wanting to find a church; we would like to come visit yours!"

That Sunday, they came to church and a month and a half later both of them became disciples of Jesus! Four months later, their daughter became the first teen woman to be baptized into Christ in our congregation.

This story is told by Chris Fuqua of Los Angeles:

Our son, Ben, was ten years old and wanted to try out for a Little League team in our area. He was drafted by the Giants, and we became "baseball parents." We were very excited about his efforts on the field, but also about getting to know parents of his teammates. It was a bit intimidating, being the new people in the baseball realm.

One family that truly amazed us was Victor and Sonia Gonzalez...and their nine kids! Sonia would come to every game—with every child. They were all extremely polite and well-behaved children. We would sit together in the stands and got to know each other a bit during the games.

At the end of the season, we had a party at a local restaurant. As we were leaving, my husband, Marty, and I walked out with Victor, and Marty asked him if he would like to come to church with us. I will never forget the way Victor's face lit up! He was so fired up! He and Sonia, now pregnant with Gonzalez number ten, walked into the service with their beautiful, large family. We took up a whole row, just by ourselves!

The Gonzalez family was overjoyed to find the kingdom of God! They studied the Bible with us, Tom and Etta McCurry and several other eager disciples. Rafael Lua and his girlfriend (now wife) Griselda, reached out to them in such an awesome way. We all shared many great meals together at each others' homes. (When you have a family of twelve over, you know you've been hospitable!)

Victor and Sonia were both baptized into Christ and they now have several important responsibilities in the Latin ministry of the Los Angeles church. They are also in the Elders Training Program.

In three years, their original six-person Bible discussion group has grown to sixty disciples!

This story told by Kim Walters of Boston:

I had never helped someone in my neighborhood become a Christian before, so when the house next door went up for sale, I decided to pray daily that a young couple who were open to the Gospel would move in.

Dave and Gail are young, newly married professionals. They moved in several months after I started praying for them. We went over to welcome them to the neighborhood and to invite them over for dessert and coffee. I started praying that a genuine friendship would develop...and it did. Dave had recently graduated from the same law school that another disciple in our group was attending, so it was a natural introduction and again, a helpful social connection.

I prayed that God was preparing their hearts for the truth. I had invited them to church several times but only received lukewarm reactions. I then invited Gail to our annual "Woman's Day." She thought it sounded interesting but was hoping to go away that weekend to celebrate her birthday. Time to pray specifically again: "God, please block any out-of-town celebration that weekend."

Gail loved Woman's Day and agreed to study the Bible. Shortly thereafter, both Gail and Dave finally came to a "Bring Your Neighbor Day" Sunday worship service. Gail liked it, but Dave did not. She made it clear that she wanted to find a church that they could enjoy together, so she started looking for another church. This was a knife in my heart because my husband does not come to church with me.

Although Dave didn't enjoy the service, he did begin to participate in studying the Bible. Soon Gail was ready to make her decision to be a disciple. Dave was close, and then, after he was hit with persecution from his family, he backed off. Gail followed suit for a few months, but eventually she worked through everything and was baptized into Christ! Six weeks later Dave was baptized into Christ!

As I write this article, Gail has just set up a study with one of her best friends from her childhood.

~~~~~

Norman Thatch, a computer analyst, is an all-American guy who loves the sport of football. When invited to take part in the New Jersey church's football league, he was amazed by the difference in the behavior of the disciples playing football and in the behavior of the nondisciples he had played with before.

Therefore, when asked to study the Bible, he agreed to do so. He became a disciple several months later. Very soon afterward, his wife was baptized into Christ. After that, his very spunky, seventy-year-old dad followed suit, and a week later his mom was also baptized into Christ. Then a financial analyst whom he met during his commute to work became a disciple. So, five people were baptized in five months from a seed planted in the football league!

~~~~~

As told by Julie Huffman of Houston:

The story of our neighborhood begins some six years ago as we searched for a house after moving to Houston. We chose our neighborhood, Cutten Green, for many reasons, among them location and racial and cultural diversity. Two months after moving in, friends of ours who are disciples, Art and Terri Rosenquist, moved in across the street with their three children. Together we carried out our mission of seeking and saving the lost through prayer and hospitality. We developed many neighborhood friendships, and one day I was introduced to a neighbor named Cynthia Taylor.

Terri and I enjoyed our new friendship with Cynthia, as we worked out together at the health club and went to late-night movies. Cynthia and her husband, Calvin, began attending our Bible discussion group, studied the Bible, and became disciples of Jesus soon after.

A few months later another family of disciples, Bobby and Carolyn Lawson, moved to our neighborhood. At about the same time a couple in the church who lives on the other side of Houston met a couple at a party who lives on our street, Melvin and Marva Little. They invited the Littles to church, and we began to study with them. They were baptized into Christ a few weeks later. A few weeks after that, Jennifer Rosenquist, Art and Terri's teenage daughter, was baptized into Christ.

We then studied with an interracial couple, Leon and La Tonya Cheyney, who live at our same house number, three blocks behind us. They were very inspired as we introduced them to family after family from our neighborhood at church. They were baptized into Christ, so in the past year God has used us to lead seven souls to Christ in Cutten Green with a racial mix of African-American, Asian, Hispanic and Caucasian! Another exciting result is that altogether we have twelve children who go to school together! Open your eyes! It can happen in your neighborhood.

Love Your Family

One of the special treasures that God gives to people on this earth is the family. The bonds of love within a family are deep and go beyond words. Of course many families experience divorce, adultery, lack of forgiveness and other painful scars. To some extent all families are faced with problems. Rather than allowing this to become an excuse for bitterness, however, the true disciple sees these needs as an opportunity to introduce his or her family to the healing power of Christ. As Christians, we are commanded to love and care for our families.

> If anyone does not provide for his relatives, and especially for his immediate family, he has denied the faith and is worse than an unbeliever (1 Timothy 5:8).

What is the most important way to love our family and provide for them? We can give them the chance to know and respond to the gospel of Christ.

To Neither Extreme

Jesus provided an outstanding example of loving his family and the families of his disciples. At the same time he was uncompromising about his commitment to God. Typically we live one of two ways: Some of us claim to love our families, while in reality we use them as an excuse for why we do not do well spiritually; others of us alienate our families by having a self-righteous attitude toward them. In fact, we avoid them and have convinced ourselves that they can never understand the kingdom of God anyway! Either way, we are denying them their chance to know God!

Although Jesus' mother certainly had her moments of frustration and misunderstanding with her son, at the end of Jesus' life Mary stood near the cross. Even as Jesus suffered in agony, he did not forget his mother.

> Near the cross of Jesus stood his mother, his mother's sister, Mary the wife of Clopas, and Mary Magdalene. When Jesus saw his mother there, and the disciple whom he loved standing nearby, he said to his mother, "Dear woman, here is your son," and to the disciple, "Here is your mother." From that time on, this disciple took her into his home (John 19:25-27).

Despite his own trials, Jesus remained aware of his mother's sorrow. His mother was a widow who was about to lose her precious and beloved first child. Even in the throes of death, Jesus made sure that his mother would be cared for. At that time, he gave his mother to his beloved disciple, John. Mary was to be John's mother. John brought her into his home as his own mother and took care of her. Godly love for our family helps us to rise above our personal hardships and continue to make an eternal difference.

Love in Action

The grace of God allowed Frank and me to take my sister-in-law and my nephew into our home after my only brother died in a tragic car accident. My sister-in-law, Masayo, and I cried many tears together the first few months she lived with us. She helped to heal the wounds of losing my little brother, because she became my sister in Christ just three months after moving in with us. My nephew, Hiroaki, became a little brother to my two daughters. Hiroaki brought laughter and smiles into our family.

God continued to work through the prayers and through the love of many Christians as Masayo grew spiritually. As a result of her faith and her effectiveness, she became a ministry intern for the Tokyo church. Now, just two years after her baptism, Masayo is leading the arts/media sector in the Tokyo church alongside her new husband, Rob Narita (who played Jesus and Simon the Sorcerer in the recent version of the UpsideDown musical). Now, the happy new family lives just down the street from us. I have personally gained a new brother, as well! It is amazing to see God's mighty hand work powerfully when we remain committed to loving our family the way God wants us to.

This victory has affected her family and my family as they see the changes in Masayo and Hiroaki. They also see the deep love that we have for each other.

Family Time

In November 1995, before all the plans were set for Masayo to move in with us, the Tokyo church planned for 1996 to have the theme "Year of the Family." Frank and I started the "Silver" or Senior Ministry. We baptized nine mothers and fathers of disciples in six months! The domino effect of parents being baptized also allowed many siblings, children and even grandparents to be baptized into Christ! Families in Tokyo were reunited and also united in Christ like never before. Christians who had neglected their families in the past began writing cards and making phone calls. Though some parents and siblings did not respond to the Bible, many family relationships with past hurts were healed that year, clearing the way for spiritual growth in the future.

The Senior Ministry is now a ministry in and of itself, and it continues to influence the entire church powerfully. In Japan the "older generation" is revered and respected by the young. They have not only added maturity to our church, but a sense of stability, as well. We are grateful for the total commitment of these senior adults in our church. Their love for God and their willingness to commute long hours to church and stay up late to study with their friends remove all excuses from our younger members.

God blesses the church and the lives of those who take care of and nurture their families. It is a basic teaching in the Bible. Let us have a renewed zeal to help our families to know Christ. No matter how we may have neglected them or failed to be bold in the past, we can repent today. God is always with us to help us—especially through our mistakes. Let us not hold back one day longer with the people we should love the most on this earth—our families!

Faith-Building Stories

In Manila, Philippines, three months pregnant at the age of eighteen and walking down the aisle toward her fiancé, Dhom, Jackie Francisco thought that this marriage would be the beginning of a dream come true. Yet, quickly she realized that it was actually the beginning of many challenges and lonely nights. Although they started and ran a successful family business and raised three children in ten years of marriage, Jackie lived with the insecurity of wondering what her husband was doing out late so many nights. His lifestyle of car racing, drinking, drugs and unfaithfulness had never changed after their wedding day. She resorted to keeping quiet and allowing herself to be the second woman instead of his wife.

Praise God that she was met by a Christian and invited to attend church and study the Bible. Jackie was baptized into Christ, even though she knew about her husband's two children with two different women outside of their marriage: She had learned to forgive him as God had forgiven her of her own immorality and bitterness.

Jackie continued to persevere and commit herself to her husband, Dhom. She was five months pregnant with their fourth child when God worked miraculously in the life of her husband. Dhom had just finished closing his store when an unknown perpetrator came from behind and stabbed him twice. He was quickly rushed to the emergency room. The knife had missed all his vital organs by less than one inch.

While recuperating in the hospital, many of Jackie's new Christian friends visited him—people he had never met before. Also, his mistress came to visit him while Jackie was by his bedside. Jackie excused herself so that they could talk. The next day his mistress came again, this time with a child of his. Jackie again excused herself so that they could talk.

After a week, Dhom was released from the hospital to recuperate for one month at home. On his first day back, Jackie asked him if they could pray together. To Jackie's surprise, he agreed. The first time they prayed together, Dhom could not keep himself from crying. They prayed together every morning for the whole month he rested. As soon as he was physically able, Jackie brought him to church. He studied the Bible that day and was baptized into Christ one week later!

Dhom recalls that week in the hospital, lying on his side because of the pain in his back. He remembers all the Christians who visited him. He had really been touched and impressed by their genuine concern. But even more so, he could not believe that Jackie was not mad at him for the arrival of his mistress at the hospital, especially with the child. He had seen for the first time in his life how much he had really hurt Jackie and how righteous she had been since she had been baptized a year earlier.

One week after his baptism, Dhom saw his brother baptized into Christ. Then his sister became a Christian, then a brother-in-law, his mother and Jackie's mother and father. With seven

Christians in the family, Dhom is now so grateful to Jackie for never giving up on him. Their marriage is now founded and built on Christ. To God be all the glory!

Bill and Becky Mapes' daughter, Rachele Gibson, became a disciple when she went to college at the University of North Carolina at Chapel Hill. Becky was a very religious person and did not respond to her daughter's attempts to reach out to her. Bill and Becky did respond, however, to Rachele's unconditional love and example of what a disciple is. Rachele's life made an impression on her parents, living in Atlanta, over a period of ten years.

After attending Rachele's wedding, the Mapes were so impressed that they came to church and began to study the Bible. In the religious world Bill and Becky had never seen what they saw in God's church. They worked through a lot of things in their characters and in their marriage and then were baptized into Christ—ten years after Rachele had become a disciple and first shared her faith with them!

Jason Estrada is a disciple in the New York City Church of Christ. He loves God and loves his large family. After years of seeing Jason grow spiritually and change his life, his mother, Cece, was inspired to study the Bible. Cece was baptized into Christ and was eager to share her new life with her large family.

She was so grateful and excited that she was determined to save her whole extended family around the country! She tracked down phone numbers of the women's ministry leaders in over twenty cities where she had family households around the US. She desired to personally help her family get in touch with the church in their areas.

In the two years after Cece became a disciple, she and Jason have led the following people to Christ: Cece's uncle Roy; Jason's son's mother, Donna; Donna's mother, Dorothy; Cece's teenage daughter Patricia; and Donna's teenage daughter Anna!

Cece and Jason are far from done yet!

As told by Nick Young of Dallas:

About five summers ago, my nephew, Jeremy, came from Colorado to stay with my family and me for six weeks. At fifteen years old he had begun to drift away from his mother, from a good conscience and into sin and rebelliousness. So we were excited about Jeremy coming into our home and felt this could be the opportunity he needed. As he lived with us and participated in the church activities, he changed immediately.

Then we went to our summer Christian youth camp. While there, Jeremy decided to become a disciple of Jesus. He started studying the Bible that week while at camp. We continued studying, and ten days after camp I baptized my nephew into Christ!

The change in his life was so radical that my sister and my mother (his mother and grandmother), though three states away, perceived his transformation merely in their phone conversations. They were so impressed that they decided to attend the church in Denver and begin studying the Bible with the women's ministry leader there and with my wife, Debbie, over the phone. In the end Debbie flew out and studied with my mom each day and my sister each evening. Five days later I drove Jeremy, along with our two children, John and Amy, to Colorado and baptized my mother and sister into Christ as disciples. It was a glorious time for our family!

A few months later they all moved to Dallas to be near us and to be a part of the Dallas church. Jeremy now is in the third year of a football scholarship at the University of Central Oklahoma. My sister lives across the street from us and leads a group of disciples. My mom, a Bible discussion group leader, works for me as my personal executive assistant. All three are very fruitful in their ministry for the Lord. Because of Jesus and the church, our family has been redeemed, and our relationships are better than ever before. Praise God for these blessings!

As told by Carol Washington of Boston:

On the night that I met David Washington I sent up a prayer that went something like this: "God, I love this boy. I know he doesn't like me now, but I know if you just allow our paths to cross again, he will. God, I want to be his wife and I know that if it is your will, I will be his wife. Please help him to be happy and most of all God, please protect him from harm until we meet again, and even after that, please protect him forever and ever...." I was sure that God would answer this prayer.

David and I did meet again, but it was eight years later at a party. That night I engaged in the most intense prayer yet. So, who do I see on my way to work the next day? None other than David himself! Eventually we became the best of friends, fell in love and moved in together.

One day my brother Darryl and his wife, Barbara, called us to tell us that they were studying the Bible with my eldest brother, Van, and his wife Shemetra. David and I thought that it was just a phase that they were going through and that they would get over it. We were dead wrong! We witnessed the radical changes in their lives; they were becoming truly happy.

The happiness that David and I thought we had did not even compare to what we saw in the lives of Darryl and Barbara. We convinced ourselves that getting married was the answer, when all along we knew that God was the answer. How did we know that? We saw the happiness in Van and Shemetra's lives, who had been disciples for years, and now we were starting to see it in Darryl and Barbara's lives. Still, we didn't eagerly seek God because we were afraid of the changes we would have to make. In fact, it wasn't until I had gotten pregnant that David and I both knew that we had to surrender our lives to God.

David and I studied the Bible with my brothers and their wives and with a few other disciples. As our convictions grew stronger, we started to change. I moved out, with no doubt in my mind that God was going to bless what we view now as such a small sacrifice. And he did! We were both baptized into Christ and were married less than two months later. To God be the glory!

When Alice Coleman of Chicago became a disciple of Jesus, she prayed constantly that her husband, Wally, would make that same decision for his life. Although he occasionally attended various church activities, that decision seemed far from him. Over the next few years, Alice tried not to be discouraged by Wally's unresponsiveness, as many disciples reached out to him. She persevered and maintained her godly example of a Christian wife, even though her husband would not see his need for God.

However, one day Wally felt overwhelmed by the breakdown in communication with his teenage son, which was greatly affecting their relationship. Out of a growing desperation, Wally asked his wife for the first time in their marriage if they could pray together to help their son. The seeds that had previously been planted were sprouting as he began to realize that in order to help his son, he would first have to become a good example himself. God was moving in his heart. He knew that it was time to start seriously studying the Bible. After making a decision to repent and become a disciple, he was baptized into Christ.

After being introduced to the church in Detroit, Michigan, by a college friend, Sherrine Eckersley was excited to see a racially diverse, young and alive church that actually obeyed the Scriptures. She began to share her newfound faith with her friends and family. Immediately after she was baptized into Christ, her husband, Rod, began studying the Bible and just ten days later was baptized into Christ. Both Rod and Sherrine joined the administrative staff in Detroit, and then later moved to Chicago, where Rod currently serves as the controller for the Midwest churches.

Sherrine's gratitude for the kingdom propelled her to invite her family to all kinds of church activities. She sought help from other Christians she knew could relate well to her family. This proved to be very effective.

Sherrie introduced her eldest sister Michele to Sharon Reed, who had similar character traits. Michele began studying the Bible and was soon baptized into Christ. After her older brother, Darius, had returned from Africa with his new wife, Angeline, Sherrine paired the couple with some disciples whom she knew could help lead them to Christ. They too began studying and were baptized into Christ. Angeline invited her sister in Africa to come live with them, hoping that she would become a disciple. After establishing some great friendships, Venna was also baptized into Christ.

Although Darius and Angeline moved to Boston, Darius made a return trip home to Michigan to study with and baptize his and Sherrine's stepfather into Christ. Immediately, Sherrine asked a close disciple friend of hers to become her mother's best friend. One year later, Darius and Angeline flew in from Boston and Rod and Sherrine from Chicago to baptize their mother into Christ. Now family reunions and holiday celebrations take on a whole new meaning!

As told by Amby Murphy of Boston:

"If you love something, let it go. If it is yours, it will come back to you. If it isn't, it never will." I have always believed that this statement expresses God's gift of free will to man. In the case of my sister, I also think it describes how she came to Christ.

Following in my footsteps, my younger sister expressed some real interest in Jesus at an early age. But when I left for college and a strong campus ministry she, as a young teen, was left in a small, lifeless church—to die spiritually.

Over the next ten years, we went our separate ways. Our friendship was strained. We did not speak about spiritual things, but I did not hide anything from her. I knew that she would have to rediscover God as an adult and this time in a true church.

After many disappointing relationships with men, Martha's heart was beginning to soften. She was living in Boston and was met by a disciple. When I learned that she was studying the Bible, I called her.

Not long after, Martha stopped studying the Bible. Instead, she went to evangelical churches in the Boston area—volunteered her time, helped their poor, tutored their immigrants. And each time she went, she would fill out a card in the pew saying: "I would like more information about your church." No one called. No one responded to her.

Then we met one night and talked for hours. We talked out her ten years of criticisms, questions and fears. I was not defensive. I did not have all the answers. I just shared with her what I had been through over the past ten years.

Martha was baptized soon after. This time, she was not baptized for me—but for Jesus. She has been fruitful in many ways. She married an awesome disciple two years ago and is expecting her first child.

Abraham Hernandez was a bright student at Loyola Marymount University. He had a dream of becoming a lawyer and really making a difference in the world. Abraham was met by disciples attending Santa Monica College, and before long he was studying the Bible. Although he wanted to be baptized, the intense persecution he received from his girlfriend, Kelly, and his sister Feli wore him down. On the day he was supposed to be baptized, he never showed up. He also stopped going to church.

About a year later, his sister Feli was working for an entertainment lawyer. Edwin Padanganan and Ernesto Saldivar, who were there on business, invited Feli to come to church for a special worship service. Feli came to church that Sunday, not realizing that it was the same church she had persecuted her brother for attending. She was moved to tears by the communion message and agreed to study the Bible. She was baptized into Christ a few weeks later.

Feli was distressed that she had previously persecuted her brother, and she called him and begged him to come back to church.

Abraham did come back, restudied the Bible and moved out of the apartment he shared with his girlfriend, Kelly. Kelly began to study and both Kelly and Abraham were baptized into Christ. Another of Feli's brothers, Moses, and a sister, Arci, were also baptized. A few months later her other brother, Chevy, was baptized. He was followed by their sister, Lourdes, six months later. Then Herman, another brother, and his wife Vanessa were baptized into Christ.

Feli also reached out to her longtime friend, Sharon Brubaker, who was baptized. Then while being sworn in as US citizens, Feli invited Alhua Cuardo to church, and she was baptized into Christ. (If you are counting, that is at least ten!) As this book was being written, Feli had just become a part of the ministry staff of the arts/media/sports ministry of the LA church.

<hr />

Christoph Widmer, a high school student from Switzerland, was introduced to disciples while visiting London. Having grown up being religious, he was impressed by how these men and women weren't just religious, but actually lived out what they taught. They invited him to return for a week-long teen ministry retreat a few months later. Christoph attended the retreat and after studying the Bible that week was baptized into Christ!

Christoph remembers, "The next day I had to return home to Switzerland, not knowing of any other disciples in the whole country. My school started again on Monday, two days after my baptism. That was quite a change! But I felt the mission that lay ahead: There was a whole country to be evangelized. I thought of how I could win my friends but was trying to be very cautious because I feared that many would oppose my new faith, which in turn could shake me. And I didn't want to stumble and fall. I didn't even tell my mom and my brothers, who I was living with, that I had become a Christian. The longer I waited, the more silly it seemed to tell all about it."

But tell his friends he did. For his next vacation, he and four friends went to visit the Munich church. Within a few months three of them had made their decisions to be baptized into Christ, in addition to another friend thirty miles away! This caused quite a stir in their village of merely 1300 people, and wild stories about their faith began to circulate. Christoph's mother began to be inundated with questions of all kinds, which she then relayed to him. For the most part, she trusted him instead of the rumors because of what she saw in his life.

Christoph's post-graduation adventure was to be a part of the Berlin mission team. Many questions were going through his mind as he prepared to leave: "How would my mom be able to become a Christian? How could my younger brother (eleven at that time) grow up to believe without my being there? Wouldn't he follow my older brother's example who still lived with my mom and who had decided to go back to our former youth group and not be a disciple?" But God had a plan to bless Christoph's sacrifice.

Christoph describes what happened: "Two years later the Zurich church was planted, which was only an hour from my family's home. My younger brother, Matthias, thirteen by this time, frequently persuaded our mom to go to church with him, but he even made the journey alone at times. My mom was also attending various denominational churches. Then one of my friends who had become a disciple earlier and who at that time was my girlfriend, Nina, asked my mom if she would like to study the Bible. She agreed and was baptized into Christ a few months later and moved the family to Zurich to be closer to the church."

Four years passed and Christoph and Nina had gotten married, been put on staff, lead the Zurich church, and then were leading the Dusseldorf church when Matthias was baptized into Christ, nine years after Christoph's first introduction to disciples! God is faithful!

—⁂—

As told by Charles Sharp, Tampa, Florida:

The longer I was a denominational minister, the more my heart longed for a real relationship with God and with true, sincere, devout disciples—those who would love unconditionally. Competition, jealousies and political maneuvers between ministers within the church began to sicken me.

One day someone named Pat Gempel telephoned us and shocked us by asking about our adopted daughter, Roxanne. At that time, Pat was a women's ministry leader and her husband, Bob, served as an elder in the Boston church. As her birth mother, Pat wanted permission to contact Roxanne. We were devastated, but reluctantly agreed. Little did I know that God was moving to bring me into that genuine relationship with him.

Within three months Roxanne Armes and her husband, Eddie, moved from Indiana to stay with the Gempels in Concord, Massachusetts. They soon studied the Bible and were baptized into Christ. We figured that such a dramatic change in faith, doctrine and experience could only mean one thing—they were being led astray by a cult. So, my wife, Marion, and I went to Boston for a two-week visit to check things out, and we were amazed by the love, joy and enthusiasm of the Christians in the worship services we attended.

Then Marion went to be with Roxanne during the delivery of her second child, Makhaila. During this time Sheila Jones studied the Bible with Marion. After Makhaila was born, Eddie called to see if I would take a weekend off to see my new granddaughter, expenses paid, for Father's Day. Arriving Friday night, I met Tom Jones who asked me if I would like to see what Marion was studying. I consented.

Tom Jones and Wyndham Shaw had cleared their schedules so they could spend time with me in the Word from 9:00 AM to 11:00 PM that Saturday, and again after the worship service at the Boston Garden on Sunday (Father's Day) from 3:00 PM until almost midnight.

I knew in my heart that I could not step on that airplane Monday morning without first being baptized into Christ. At 1:15 AM on Monday many disciples shared in the miracle of God. Bob Gempel baptized me into Christ, and then I baptized Marion into Christ! We then studied the Bible with Marion's ninety-six-year-old mother, who was baptized into Christ a month after we were. She went to be with Jesus six months later.

Marion and I moved to Detroit, Michigan, and while in the Detroit church, Marion was instrumental in studying the Bible with a friend who was baptized into Christ in the cold, fall waters of Lake Michigan.

We later moved to Florida and were a part of the new Greater Tampa Bay church at its inception and have helped to see it grow. And God is more precious to us now than ever before!

As told by Astrid Herrmann of Berlin:

My husband, Thomas, and I are Germans and moved as newly-weds to the States. We met disciples in the Chicago church, studied the Bible and were baptized into Christ only six weeks after our wedding. For the first time in my life, I learned to focus on others, instead of on myself.

It was hard to reach out to our immediate family, since they all live in Germany, and we were merely seeing them twice a year. During one visit I had a talk with my younger brother, Robert (Hueber), with whom I had not had a close relationship since childhood. While becoming a Christian, I had worked through some family issues and thought perhaps my brother might be struggling with the same things.

My brother and his wife, Katja, had just had their second child and seemed happy and content with their little family. We were raised as atheists with no interest in spiritual matters, so I thought that my brother would be the last person who would possibly be open. But I longed to share my new convictions and to get closer to him again.

Robert's response to my sharing was amazing. He started opening up and immediately poured out his heart. He told me that he was going through a very hard time finding his place in life and was struggling with a rather severe depression. I was stunned by his unexpected openness, and we talked a lot that day. Sadly, we had to go back to the US, so we could not go into any detail. I just shared how Jesus' love has helped me and tried to give him some hope.

Six weeks later, the phone rang in our home in Chicago. It was the middle of the night in Germany, and I was alarmed when I realized that it was my brother. His depression and hopelessness had gotten worse, and nothing seemed to help. He told me that he had lost weight and was hardly able to work. He cried on the phone, and so did his wife. Thoughts of what I could do raced through my mind. I was 4000 miles away and my parents were on vacation— and I was not sure that they would understand his depression. I asked my brother and his wife if they would meet with some disciples from the Munich church, and they were open to that. In spite of his humanistic, scientific background, my brother was at the point where he was open to hear about God's message of hope for mankind.

Robert and a brother on the staff of the Munich church talked on the phone the very next day, and he gave Robert his first scriptures ever to read, introducing him to the principle of an infinite God with infinite wisdom. I took a vacation from work and flew to Germany two days later on a secret mission. I met my brother and his family in Munich where we had a counseling session with a German couple. My brother and his family stayed one month in Munich on an unpaid leave of absence.

Over the course of the next six months, Robert and Katja commuted four hours to study the Bible. God's word and the friendships with Christians worked in their hearts and minds. Back in the States, we kept in close contact with them and with people in the Munich church. The brothers and sisters in Chicago helped us through those difficult, emotional times. Our phone bill was sky high, and our knees hurt, but it was worth it! They were baptized into Christ!

Thomas and I now live in Berlin, and Robert and Katja are some of our best friends. They lead a Bible discussion group and oversee the children's ministry in the Dusseldorf church. They have been blessed with three children.

As told by Jeanne Washington of Boston:

Many years ago my daughter Deena began studying the Bible while she was a senior in high school. I was very supportive of her decision to study and later to be baptized into Christ. The day before her baptism several people from church came to our home

to discuss Deena's decision and the baptism itself with my husband, Bill, and me. I was feeling a lot, including, "How could my
seventeen-year-old daughter possibly know that baptism is what
she needs?"

Bill and I attended Deena's baptism, and I began to realize
that I had never asked Deena much about what she was learning
about God and how her Bible studies were going. At that time I was
just grateful that she was not leading a promiscuous life, as many
young girls were doing. She was a good student athlete who was
not doing drugs.

I did not understand Deena's desire and passion for her personal relationship with God and for meeting with the disciples. I
thought, "Wasn't church on Sunday enough?"

Deena began attending a major university and moved on campus due to the partial athletic scholarship she was awarded for
track and field. She became a part of the campus ministry, and my
concerns about the church began to escalate. I began to persecute
my own child because of negative things I heard about the church.
Someone from the university sent me literature on how the church
had a history of destroying the lives of young people and their
families. I bought into the propaganda and began to fear for Deena's
well-being and safety.

I continued to persecute my daughter and shared with her all
the negative things I was told. You can imagine the division that
occurred in our relationship. I was certain that Deena was undergo-
ing some mind control process and that she was lost to me forever.
Never once during this time did I address my own need for spiritual
growth. Never did I ask Deena to open the Bible and share with me
what she was learning. I never asked if I could pray with her or go to
church with her. Deena did all of the initiating by inviting me to
many church events and worship services. Although I did attend a
few church functions, I would not go to church.

On one Mother's Day Deena asked me to attend church because she wanted to share about me. I told her "No!" This rejection hurt her deeply, but she never stopped loving me. I was
ashamed of my decision and began to realize that her heart and

love for me emulated the heart and love that Jesus has for lost souls like me.

My heart began to soften and God was preparing me for something greater: my personal walk and relationship with him! When I attended the church's Christmas program with Deena, something miraculous happened to me. I wept openly through most of the program. I began to attend church regularly and soon after, studied the Bible. I was beginning to comprehend and respect what my daughter had known for a long time. I was baptized into Christ seven years after my daughter. I am so grateful for God's—and my daughter's—unconditional love!

This story is adapted from Our Beginning
by Kay Summers McKean:

An extraordinary woman was baptized into Christ in Paris in 1996. This woman's husband had been unfaithful to her in the past, and unfortunately became infected with HIV. Knowing that he carried this deadly disease, he had sexual relations with his wife without informing her of the danger. Later, when she contracted AIDS, the truth came out. Everyone in the family was infuriated by the father and ostracized him for what he had done to his wife.

Everyone, that is, except one of his daughters, who happens to be a disciple. She had compassion on her father, and against the objections of the rest of the family, continued to love him and reach out to him. Her devotion to him touched him and opened his heart to the gospel. When he became ill, he was all the more eager to get his life right with God and to ask for forgiveness from his wife. He was baptized into Christ shortly before his death.

His wife had noticed all the changes in her husband and saw the unconditional love of her daughter. She too was touched and wanted to learn about Jesus. When it seemed that her death was drawing near, she asked to leave the hospital—to get baptized into Christ before hundreds at a European conference. Her body was weak, but she emerged from the water with arms held high in victory. Her new birth was witnessed by disciples around the world via video.

Her health eventually stabilized, and she is currently on a mission team, spreading the good news of love and forgiveness!

As told by Alex Lynn of Dallas, Texas:

My wife, Debbie, and I are leaders of a group of disciples in the church in Dallas/Ft. Worth, and we have been in the kingdom for about two years. One of the thrills of being in the kingdom is watching God work through us and make an eternal impact in the lives of the people we touch: We are now a conduit for God's love and wisdom.

Until about two years ago, my wife and I were in a traditional, denominational church for decades. We thought that our family was secure in Christ and that we were doing our utmost to raise our children in the nurture and admonition of the Lord.

The scripture that could describe our story is 1 Corinthians 1:27-30. While still in our arrogance, it took a son becoming involved in the homosexual lifestyle to crush our pride, to teach us about unconditional love and to put our focus on eternal issues. God used that brutal lesson to prepare us for finding his kingdom.

Our next challenge was that our youngest daughter became pregnant while in a relationship with a young man who had turned his back on his faith. Because of the lesson in love that we had already learned, my wife and I could love the young man with the idea of helping him to come back to God. In trying to understand him, we discovered that he previously was a part of the Dallas/Ft. Worth church. Through our work with him we came in contact with disciples in that church. After more Bible study we realized that we had never become disciples of Jesus, despite our religious background. We were then baptized into Christ!

As of this writing, three of our four children are disciples and are doing well spiritually. (Our youngest daughter is now coleading a Bible discussion group with the restored father of our grandson.) God is awesome!

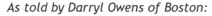

As told by Darryl Owens of Boston:

On February 24,1984, my older brother, Van, came home and told me his good news: He had been baptized into Christ. I could not understand why someone so young (nineteen) would give up everything before he had the chance to experience anything.

My brother began to study the Bible with me, but my heart was not ready to respond to Jesus' call. I decided that all of the sin that I had not yet experienced—and all of the sin that I was currently involved in—was more appealing than Christianity.

I graduated from high school and went to Boston University where my brother was a junior. My heart was so hard by that time that all of the genuine love and excitement that I saw in those campus disciples was distorted in my own mind: I looked at them as plastic and annoying. Little did I know that they were probably the most sincere people that I had ever met.

Years later I met and fell in love with an incredible woman, but our relationship was weak. I had thought that a woman in my life would fill up the void in my heart that I had felt as long as I could remember. I realized very quickly that she did not fill it. We both felt it and thought we could fix it by living together. When that did not work, we decided to get married. After the honeymoon was over, we found ourselves still very much in love but very much in need of help.

After being married for a few months, my wife, Barbara, lost two of her grandparents within forty days of one another. She was grief stricken, and I was at a loss as to how to help her. I figured that we could start reading the Bible together, but we understood little. I knew who to call for help: Van. He and his wife, Shemetra, helped us to understand Jesus and his love for us.

On February 24, 1994, exactly ten years to the day after my brother's baptism into Christ, my wife and I were baptized into Christ!

Be an Example on the Job

As Jesus walked by the Sea of Galilee, he saw Simon and his brother Andrew casting a net into the lake, for they were fishermen. "Come, follow me," Jesus said, "and I will make you fishers of men." At once they left their nets and followed him.

When he had gone a little farther, he saw James son of Zebedee and his brother John in a boat, preparing their nets. Without delay he called them, and they left their father Zebedee in the boat with the hired men and followed him.

Mark 1:16-20

"I'm so busy."

"I have no time."

"You don't understand, Frank, because you don't have a real job."

Well, I have never read in the Scriptures that preaching the gospel was anything less than a lot of work—the phrase "blood, sweat and tears" comes to mind—but I do happen to know of a few guys who had what some might call real jobs.

You may have heard of them. Peter. Andrew. James. John. Don't forget Levi, also known as Matthew.

As he walked along, he saw Levi son of Alphaeus sitting at the tax collector's booth. [That was his job.] "Follow me," Jesus told him, and Levi got up and followed him (Mark 2:14).

Jesus did not do anything by chance, and his timing in calling his first disciples, his core leadership, to total commitment was certainly no accident. Notice the common denominator: "casting a net into the lake"; "preparing their nets"; and "sitting at the tax collector's booth."

Do you see a pattern emerging? Jesus purposefully and deliberately called his disciples at the most inconvenient, disruptive time imaginable: while they were at work! Even the verb tense shows that they were not just sitting around on the job, but in the middle of activity. After Jesus had spent hours and days developing his relationship with them, teaching and befriending them, he now asked for a radical decision. Which would it be: their work or his work? Their careers or his purpose? Selfish ambition or noble ambition? No time for wavering, excuses or compromise. Jesus demanded their absolute commitment to be what he was—a fisher of men.

Our Christian lives are not pies to be sliced up among a list of priorities. No matter how many hats we may wear, we always have but one ultimate mission. Is your mission clear today?

Follow Jesus

My friend, Michitaka, had just become a Christian. He was working at the prestigious Kyodo News Agency and wanted to make an impact for Christ. He asked me what to do. At the time, my Japanese linguistic ability was still very limited, so I skipped the complicated points and settled on something I could confidently communicate. I simply replied, "Always imagine, What would Jesus do? How would he treat this person? How would he act in this situation? Then do it." Just a three- or four-month-old disciple, Michitaka did not know enough to accuse me of oversimplification or being naïve. In fact, he was quite satisfied with the answer. As a result, several of his coworkers came to church, studied the Bible and one was baptized into Christ a few months later.

Today, Michitaka is an evangelist in the Tokyo church and leads a large ministry primarily composed of single professionals. His advice has not changed because it works: "Follow Jesus. Do what he would do."

Are You Like Jesus?

"Come, follow me." Become like Jesus. Imitate his joy, his compassion, his peace, his faithfulness, his kindness and his self-control (Galatians 5:22). In every exciting victory story about the workplace that I have heard (and there are many!), this is where it always began. Go against the grain and encourage rather than grumble. Surprise the office by making someone's birthday special. Show them your family photos, and do some bragging about your spouse. Take the time to talk about more than the latest gossip. Learn humbly from those more skilled than you. Make it a point to keep your word, complete your assignments and be a light. Never make excuses.

Jesus was an opinion leader. Becoming like him requires more than being a nice piece of office furniture that no one notices and that never gets in the way. As a Christian, your daily desire to grow—to become more encouraging, more disciplined, more joyful—should lead to an increasing influence in those who spend hours around you every week. The lessons you learn in the church about spiritual leadership should be utilized in order to make a difference in the worldliness of your working environment. Remember Jesus, and seize your opportunities!

All the Time You Need

"I don't have time to be fruitful." Do you believe that our God is in control? You probably spend forty to sixty hours each week at work. Outside of sleep, that is about one-third of your time. It occupies your focus and energies. How do you view that huge portion of your life? Is that time simply lost to the kingdom and its mission? Or is that time an opportunity to fulfill your mission? In Tokyo, where office workers must often arrive each day before 9:00 am and stay past 7:00 pm (plus an average of two hours daily commuting time!), this is a critical issue.

Hiroshige graduated from a famous university in Tokyo where he had become a disciple during his freshman year. He had eagerly anticipated serving God in an influential job. Despite his initially high expectations, Hiroshige found himself caught in the Japanese economic recession and was turned down for all of his first choices. Finally, he landed a job with a small company in an industry he knew nothing about. While many might have been bitter at the prospect of having to compromise their grand dreams, Hiroshige believed that God had a purpose for him.

As a college student, Hiroshige had been free to spend hours a day inviting people to church and studying the Bible with them. As an employee of a small, expanding company, he was suddenly working from morning till night, sometimes six days a week. Interestingly enough, however, it was after he began spending long hours at work that he had perhaps his greatest eternal impact—because his workplace became his opportunity to shine like Christ rather than his excuse to hide the light.

Little did Hiroshige know that prior to his arrival at the firm, the office had been experiencing internal strife and turmoil. As a result, the working atmosphere had been dark and negative for months. Hiroshige's impact was almost immediate. His cheerful willingness to serve others and his positive attitude toward work were in stark contrast to the general mood and quickly drew attention. One coworker who later came to church recalled hearing Hiroshige singing joyfully to himself while walking to work one morning. (Most of us sing on our way home!)

Later, God's incredible plan was more completely revealed when the president of the company, her husband, her daughter and her son-in-law were all baptized into Christ. They now form a tremendous spiritual pillar for our married ministry in the Tokyo church. As for the office, many are now disciples and the atmosphere has completely changed. Our jobs must never represent "lost time" to the mission of the church. By being like Jesus we can turn our workplace into an opportunity for us to impact others on a daily, intensive basis.

Fishers of Men

𝒪 Obviously, we switch companies and change jobs for a myriad of reasons, not the least of which is to advance our careers. But as the writer of Proverbs says, "In his heart a man plans his course, but the Lord determines his steps" (16:9). God doesn't work by chance! You have a spiritual, eternal reason for being at your workplace. If you have the heart of Christ, then the ultimate purpose for every job you hold is clear: to be a fisher of men. 𝒪

Over the centuries, one of the most dangerous misconceptions that has doomed almost every "Christian" group in Japan thus far is the idea that there is a difference in commitment and mission between the ministry staff of the church and the rest of the membership. Biblically, this is false doctrine. While the paid staff is to certainly lead by example and use their time to the utmost in advancing the cause of Christ, every disciple is to view his or her life as that of a missionary. Thus, your workplace is your mission field. Few others will ever touch this field, and you may very well be your office staff's only chance to hear the true message of salvation.

When I first took the mission team to Cambodia in 1992, that nation had been through over twenty-five years of constant civil war. Millions had seen family members butchered, and everyone had lived with the constant fear of violent betrayal. I noticed that it was easy for the mission team members to be influenced by this atmosphere of suspicion and coldness. Of course, the Cambodians themselves did not expect us to pay much attention to their personal needs or to express kindness or compassion. It bothered me that some of our team were affected by this and had begun to subtly change. Finally, I led a devotional in which I challenged all the disciples to meditate on this thought: You are the only Jesus they will ever see. How impressive is your humility, your sincerity, your love? Does your life call people to follow Christ? Are you desperate to see them saved? •

Perhaps we should organize mission team send-offs for everyone who goes into a new workplace! Then we might truly understand. You are the missionary. What does your workplace see? Does your life call them to follow Jesus? How desperate are you to see them saved? God does not respect or accept two-faced discipleship in which our Christianity is reserved for the safe refuge of the fellowship. Your workplace is your spiritual mission field. God doesn't work by chance. You have been sent there for an eternal reason.

Stand Firm

Lastly—never, never, never be ashamed of being a Christian! Share openly and joyfully about the many experiences and blessings you enjoy as a disciple. And don't compromise.

Recently, a sister called and shared in a tearful voice that she had just been fired. The president of her company had become exasperated with her because of her continued refusal to lie to her clients. I was impressed by the fact that this sister felt worse for her boss' hard heart than she did about losing her job. As I read to her scriptures about how proud God was of her Christian stance, she was encouraged and actually became excited about where God would lead her next.

If the workplace is truly your mission field, then be prepared for those who simply will not be open. Just as Jesus told his disciples to shake the dust off their sandals from towns that were not open, and just as Paul had to sometimes move on to the next city, you may also find yourself forced to make changes in order to maintain your commitment to God. If or when that day comes, remember the goal: to be like Christ, reaching as many as possible. Secure in those convictions, refuse to compromise and refuse to become bitter. Accept it as another step in your quest to follow Jesus. Remember, God doesn't work by chance! There must be others elsewhere who also need to hear.

So, whatever you may do for a living, I leave you this challenge: Get a real job! One that demands your ultimate efforts to be like Christ and one that rewards you with an eternal impact. Be a fisher of men!

Faith-Building Stories

As told by James Sulewski:

Paul Hagerty was the courier for the talent agency for which I worked. He came in every day to pick up our photo submissions that would go to casting directors for consideration. As a talent agent, I was always focused on reaching out to the talent, until one day I got into a conversation with Paul. He looked "closed" to my worldly eyes, but God could see what I could not.

Paul came to a church service the following Sunday. He was blown away by the talent, spirituality and love he saw in the worship service for arts and media professionals. After the service, I sat down with Paul to get to know him better. I found out that he had a degree in theater from UCLA, and his dream was to run a "Christian" theater group. He was already seeing the possibilities for that dream at the worship service and wanted to know how to become a member! Needless to say, I was fired up to show Paul God's plan for our lives.

As we began to study the Bible together, Paul saw how much he had religion in his life, but not the plan of Jesus—discipleship. Paul had led a "good moral life." He was devoted to being close to God; he read the Bible daily and prayed. But as he studied out what it means to become a true disciple of Jesus, his heart was convicted, and he was baptized into Christ shortly thereafter.

Paul has had to endure persecution from his family: His father was a former pastor and his brother was very religious. I believe this has helped Paul develop deep convictions about God's kingdom and his plan for our lives. Paul has excelled as a disciple. He now leads a group of disciples in the arts/media/sports ministry of the Los Angeles church.

Paul is a very talented actor, as well, and has been a part of several productions in the kingdom, most recently KNN's "A Call to Fish." This summer he will be the West Coast director for the HOPE Youth Corps in LA and San Francisco.

Cheryl Payne is a member of the New York City Church of Christ. She is also a chemical engineer working for Con Edison. Cheryl has been a disciple for about seven years and has always wanted to be effective and fruitful.

On the day that Cheryl invited her boss to attend church, she doubted that she would come. What Cheryl did not realize, however, was that her boss was feeling as though the bottom had dropped out of her life—even to the point of contemplating suicide the weekend before Cheryl's invitation. It took eight months, but Cheryl's boss finally accepted the invitation and came to church. She loved church and studied the Bible. Ten days later, Cheryl's boss was baptized into Christ!

Life is different now on the job. Her boss told Cheryl later that she was watching Cheryl during those eight months and was impressed by her job performance. That is what greatly influenced her to eventually accept Cheryl's invitation and to become a disciple of Jesus Christ!

Sean Holland's first impression of the kingdom was the baptism of his manager at the time, Calvin Mason. Sean was amazed: "There were twenty-five people sharing about Calvin, and all said something positive: how he touched them, how he changed, what he sacrificed...and I realized that I didn't know five people that would say something nice about me." From that day on nothing would ever be the same in Sean's life. On his way home this actor/ rapper with the tough image broke down crying.

Sean came home to his girlfriend, Sidonie, and opened up. For the first time in their relationship he was completely honest, admitting to his cheating and his lies, and saying, "I want to change; I want to get right with God." Both went to church the next day. Sean and Sidonie both studied the Bible in a week and a half and were baptized into Christ and married on the same day!

With the same fervor that had fueled his striving to "make it in the business," Sean threw himself into the life of a disciple. To support his family while pursuing his acting career, he worked for minimum wage at a children's amusement park. "I just trusted God with everything," Sean simply says. His trust has been rewarded. Now he is one of the stars (series regulars) of the popular television show Clueless. He has appeared in films and on talk shows and is probably the only celebrity in Hollywood who refuses to have an agent or manager. Sean says, "I just don't want them to take credit for what God does for me."

Sean has led his mom, his brother-in-law and many of his friends, two of whom are actors, to Christ.

As told by Jeff Johnston of Springfield, Massachusetts:
After spending a year and a half on the Burlington, Vermont mission team, I came back to Massachusetts as a man in need of

help. I am sorry to say I was convinced that my opportunity for being a man of impact had come and gone. God, however, was far from finished with me!

After working for a while for a certain company, I was transferred to an office where Matthew Kane had been the manager for the previous nine months. When I first invited Matthew to church, he seemed a little apprehensive. He had been told by another employee that I was in a cult. He did, however, come to church after only the second time I asked him. He was, to put it mildly, blown away. He started studying right away and was baptized into Christ within three weeks.

From my first day on the job I wanted Matt to feel as though he could trust me with anything. Without that trust, it would be too difficult for an employer to be humble enough to allow himself to be taught anything about his personal life. He has been perhaps the most humble man I have ever known. I thought he might want to study with some of the other brothers so that he could feel more comfortable opening up his heart and not be under the impression that I would hold anything against him. That never became an issue. He was eager to deal with his relationship with God and the sin in his life. Matt has been a joy to my heart and a reminder to me that God is not done with me yet.

David and Jennifer were living together. He worked at an auto body shop as a mechanic, and she also worked full time. He worked with a disciple whom he persecuted, laughed at and mocked for at least three years. He literally would blow smoke in his face! Jennifer was not open either; she thought everything was fine in their lives.

Then one day their lives fell apart due to unfaithfulness in the relationship. They knew they needed help, so David approached the disciple on his job, saying, "I want to go to church with you." Both David and Jennifer went, loved it and studied the Bible. They discontinued living together, were baptized into Christ, and were eventually married. Today they lead a group of disciples in the New Jersey church!

Jeff Lamotte had moved to St. Louis to work for a Fortune 500 company. Jeff's wife, Andrea, had been searching for a church home in the area, but Jeff, unmotivated because of past religious hypocrisy, usually stayed home.

Soon after his arrival in St. Louis, Jeff was invited to church by a coworker, Malvin Warrick. Though agreeing to visit soon, the Lamottes did not attend. However, God was not about to give up his pursuit of the Lamottes, and soon Jeff was invited to play in a basketball tournament with Malvin and two other disciples. Being a former college ballplayer, Jeff accepted the invitation. During the course of the tournament, Jeff noticed something different— something real and refreshing about the relationships the three disciples had with one another, but he could not determine exactly what it was.

Finally, Jeff and Andrea attended church and were blown away by the diversity and excitement they witnessed that day. They both began to study the Bible, and Malvin baptized Jeff into Christ; then Jeff baptized Andrea into Christ.

Jeff's new goal was to help one of his coworkers become a Christian. At a company picnic, Jeff met Reggie Davis. They discovered that they had much in common: same age, same number of children and an interest in sports. The Davises came to dinner and then two weeks later attended a worship service at the St. Louis church. After a period of a few months, Reggie and his wife, Juanette, were both baptized into Christ, and they grew to be leaders in the St. Louis church. Within the next three years, the Lamottes grew to be leaders and staff members of the St. Louis church.

As told by Irene Valente of Boston:

Being an incredibly shy person, I always had trouble making friends. In high school the people I found easiest to befriend were the wildest ones. Although I managed to do well in school and was a cheerleader, I "partied" a lot, abusing both alcohol and drugs.

After high school I moved to Texas with my boyfriend to start over, but it turned out to be my worst year ever. I planned to work for a year and then attend the University of Texas, but we got involved in the punk-rock scene there. I remember one night in particular coming home after an all-night party involving some serious drugs, all hyped up. I sat chain smoking cigarettes at the kitchen table with my roommate, watching a cockroach crawl around the table, simply in despair over the pit my life was in. But I felt I could do nothing about it.

Finally, I decided to move back home to Scituate, Massachusetts, to try to pull myself together. I took a fairly uneventful semester at the University of Massachusetts in Boston and broke up with my boyfriend. However, I could not get rid of all the terrible memories or the guilt I felt. I actually wished that I just could die and be born again.

That summer, at the age of nineteen, I landed a job as a secretary that I really was not qualified for. I remember thinking, "This is from God." I had only worked there for a few weeks when a disciple invited me to a Bible discussion group in Watertown. Although it was made up of married couples with children and I was an entering freshman at the Massachusetts College of Art, I felt so welcomed. I saw that they had answers—to everything. When asked to study the Bible, I jumped at the chance. Every Thursday night, I went to the Bible discussion group, studied the Bible and stayed overnight with a family there. It was so awesome—like another world!

About six weeks after first attending, I was baptized into Christ! Six years later I was married, and my husband and I are presently on the Boston church staff. We have two fabulous children: Dominic, age five, and Eliza, age two.

⎯⬤⎯

While Dr. Dave Traver was the medical director of HOPE worldwide in the Philippines, he was introduced to a doctor named Jun Pablo, who was quite well-known for his medical clinics for the poor in the city slums. They shared a mutual respect for one another's work on behalf of the needy. After building a great relationship with Dave and John Bringardner, Jun began attending church and studying the Bible. Shortly thereafter, Jun was baptized into Christ.

Having learned the power of being an excellent example on the job from Dave and John, Jun was determined to do the same. He was working as the doctor in the clinic of the premier hotel in the Philippines. He imitated those brothers in the Lord and gained a great reputation in the hotel as one who was always giving, joyful, compassionate and extremely knowledgeable in the medical field. This reputation helped to draw people to Christ. He studied the Bible with a man who worked as a fitness instructor in the hotel. He became a Christian, then five others were shared with who also decided to be baptized into Christ!

After that, Jun reached out to one of the managers at the hotel and she, too, was added to the Lord. Then another doctor that Jun hired in the clinic studied the Bible and became a Christian. Jun now serves as a part-time doctor at the hotel and is on the staff of the Manila church!

As told by Van Owens of Boston:

Since I wanted to find someone to be my best friend, I was initially very pleased when I began to hit it off with a guy in my English literature class at Boston University. Gradually, though, my skeptical side took over, and I began to be suspicious. "Nobody," I thought, "could really be that friendly unless he wanted something." I figured that he was either going to attempt to sell me something or was going to try to convert me to some religion. After we had known each other for a couple of weeks, he invited me to church. This was deeply disappointing to me. As soon as I told him that I was not interested with a resounding, "No, thank you; I'm all set," I thought he would go sit next to some other, more promising prospect for conversion. He didn't move, and I realized that he was truly interested in me as a friend and not just as a warm body to fill pews and collection plates. This moved me and made me want to go to church with him.

The experience was nothing less than spectacular! I couldn't believe that there were so many different races of people—and so many young people who were sincerely devoted to God. And the preaching: I had never heard, understood and been so convicted by the gospel in all of the many times I had attended churches in the past.

I began to study the Bible, and these guys became the best friends I ever had. In addition to studying, we played football and ultimate Frisbee and pulled all-nighters in the library. I was baptized on a Friday night, merely ten days after my first visit to church.

God has bestowed far too many blessings upon me in the fourteen years since that night! Six years later I married Shemetra Epps, the girl of my dreams. God has worked wonderfully through us and has allowed us to lead many to Christ: my brother Darryl and his wife, Barbara; my sister Carol and her husband, David; Shemetra's mom, Lois; Shemetra's brother John; and her grandmother Bessie (who's up in heaven right now keeping the chicken warm for us!).

"A new cult has entered the Philippines." That was the all-too-common buzz phrase used in the popular circles during the height of the persecution in Manila. Every newspaper and television network jumped on the bandwagon, as seemingly all of Manila focused their gossip and coffee table talks on the radical disciples based at the country's premier university, the University of the Philippines at Diliman.

Jaffy Azarraga, a writer for *The Philippine Collegian* (the UP campus newspaper), wrote articles about the church, railing against the disciples for their commitment and their teachings. As a persecutor, his goal was to destroy the church, but little did he know that the disciples prayed for him to know the truth.

A few years passed, and Jaffy entered the UP College of Law. He went to work in a university law office. There, he got to know Rommel Casis, a fellow working student and a disciple of Jesus. Rommel's commitment to the church was widely talked about by the students—including Jaffy—but his example left them no room to talk about anything else.

Being one of the top five students in the college, Rommel was inducted into the Order of the Purple Feather, an honor society reserved for those on the dean's list. He was the captain of the varsity debate team, which represented the country during an international debate in Malaysia. As a working student, Rommel's performance in the office was disciplined and excellent. As time went on, Jaffy befriended Rommel, who always seemed to be working hard to have a "positive attitude."

In boldness, faith and confidence, Rommel invited Jaffy to church, and miraculously, Jaffy accepted. Upon arrival, Jaffy found a group of people far different from what he had been led to believe he would find. Shortly thereafter, he studied the Bible and was baptized into Christ!

In a poignant testimonial before his baptism, Jaffy apologized to the church, tearfully asking for forgiveness from those whose faith he had harmed; and he thanked God for his friend Rommel. At the Sunday worship service when Jaffy was baptized into Christ, all praised God as they witnessed how God had used prayer, faith, love and excellence to work an incredible miracle of salvation!

Love the Poor

> A man with leprosy came to him and begged him on his knees.
> "If you are willing, you can make me clean."
> Filled with compassion, Jesus reached out his hand and touched
> the man. "I am willing," he said. "Be clean!"
>
> Mark 1:40-41

Among a people facing the gritty realities of daily life, Jesus understood that showing God's compassion for them in practical terms was necessary for opening their hearts to his eternal message about salvation. But this was not a method of evangelism; Jesus was genuinely concerned about this man's needs. This was not a duty. "I am willing!" Jesus declared.

Willingness

I remember our first trip to Cambodia to scout out the land for mission work in early 1992. The Communist government still ran Phnom Penh, but the Khmer Rouge held sway in the western countryside. Cambodia had been embroiled in civil war for over two decades, an ugly conflict which had witnessed the complete dismantling of a nation's infrastructure and one of the worst cases of genocide of the twentieth century.

On a sizzling hot afternoon several brothers and I rode motorbikes to the national pediatric hospital, located on the main highway to the airport. We quickly realized that in this nation where brother had killed brother, where land mines outnumbered people (an estimated ten million!), and where to trust someone could cost you your life, it would take showing the compassion of Christ in action in order for people to believe that such love really exists.

As we walked through the corridors of the hospital, I was taken aback by what I saw: almost two hundred children in a facility built for fifty; bandaged infants with glazed eyes lying on dirty straw mats in the hallways; mothers desperately trying to comfort their feverish loved ones; filth and flies everywhere.

Thinking that I, this foreigner, must be a doctor, one mother suddenly held up her child, perhaps three years old, and began to tearfully plead with me. Although I spoke no Cambodian, her request was as plain as day: "Help my child. Please, help my child!" How powerless I felt that afternoon! How intensely I felt the pain of this mother whose child was the same age as my daughter back in Tokyo.

In the next room, a woman sat weeping on a straw mat—alone. Again, no words were necessary to convey the tragic loss that had just taken place in her life.

As we walked out the door into the blinding afternoon sun, the brothers and I were silent in thought, but our hearts were churning with emotion. We had no practical idea about how we could help. But at that moment, "charity work" ceased to be a method or a duty of discipleship. Our hearts were genuinely moved, and we were absolutely willing.

A Character Issue

Despite the brevity of Mark's description, the heart of Jesus flows from every phrase:

Filled with compassion...
Jesus reached out his hand and touched the man.
"I am willing."

"Compassion" in the English language is the combination of the prefix "com-" which means "with, together" and the word "passion," which has to do with feelings and emotions. In other words, "compassion" means sharing in the emotions of another person and feeling what they feel from their perspective. In the original Greek, the word splanchnizomai denotes being "moved as to one's innards...to yearn with compassion." When Jesus met the leper, he understood his rejection, felt his longing for acceptance and sensed his desperation. And then Jesus acted.

For a disciple of Jesus, helping the poor can never be reduced to a mere expression of pity in which a superior condescendingly helps an inferior. Yes, Jesus was superior in every way to the leper—and to us—but the Bible repeatedly reminds us that he personally felt our temptations, sufferings and struggles. He did more than pity us. He had compassion for us.

Loving the poor is not a task to be started and completed on a Saturday afternoon, nor can we merely donate money and say that we have done our "duty." It is a character trait that we must allow God to disciple into us. We help because we seek to understand. We love because we know how much we need to be loved. We are not superior. We have simply been blessed by God, and now we want to reach out and touch the lives of others. Out of compassion, we must act.

"I am willing." Are you? When the announcement is made for the next immunization drive, the hospital visit, the inner-city cleanup, will you be willing? When the call is made to financially support our brothers and sisters who are laboring among the poor, will you be willing? Oh sure, you would like to do something. You feel pity (and maybe a little guilt) every time you see those horrible pictures or drive by those bleak neighborhoods. But do you have compassion? If that were your child, your brother, your mother...would you be too busy? Too strapped? Or would you be willing?

How about this: What if it were Jesus?

> "The King will reply, 'I tell you the truth, whatever you did for one of the least of these brothers of mine, you did for me'" (Matthew 25:40).

What a privilege to feed, to comfort and to support Jesus. We have the opportunity: Are you willing?

Divine Intervention

Several years after my first visit to Phnom Penh, God moved miraculously to open the door for the founding of the King Sihanouk Hospital—Center of HOPE in that same city. In the fall of 1995, I had become friends with Bernard Krisher, the former Tokyo bureau chief of Newsweek magazine and current head of a Japanese relief organization. Through his help, HOPE worldwide was able to send supplies to the destitute flood victims of North Korea.

Over the next months, I learned that Bernie was a close, personal friend of the popular king of Cambodia, Norodom Sihanouk. As such, he had been granted land in the middle of Phnom Penh, had raised funds and had managed to construct an excellent medical facility. But he had a huge problem: He had no staff and no experience in running a hospital.

By June, a mutual agreement to staff, supply and run the hospital had been signed by Robert Gempel, president of HOPE worldwide, Bernie's organization and a philanthropic Japanese donor. By September, Dr. Graham Ogle, Mark Remijan and their families had moved from New Guinea and Manila, respectively, in order to oversee the hospital's start-up. By December 1996, the doors to the King Sihanouk Hospital—Center of HOPE (SHCH) were opened to the poor of Cambodia.

The SHCH has become a refuge of true hope available to every Cambodian: excellent medical care and, more importantly, love and respect are completely free of charge. The rest is history, an amazing history that continues to be written today. Space does not permit an adequate explanation of all the incredible miracles that have occurred, nor does it allow a sufficient rendering of the heroic sacrifices of the hospital's Christian staff.

Whenever I visit or hear of the daily victories taking place at HOPE worldwide projects around the globe, I am filled with joy. When I hear of an orphan getting the chance to grow up in a Christian family, I am fired up! When it's time to financially support the hospital in Phnom Penh...I am willing! I am thankful for the chance! The hopelessness and helplessness I felt on that afternoon many years ago is gone. What an honor, what a privilege to be used by God, even in a small way, to reach out and help someone feel the compassion of God.

Fruitful Labor

> He upholds the cause of the oppressed
> > and gives food to the hungry.
> The Lord sets prisoners free,
> > the Lord gives sight to the blind,
> the Lord lifts up those who are bowed down,
> > the Lord loves the righteous.
> The Lord watches over the alien
> > and sustains the fatherless and the widow,
> > but he frustrates the ways of the wicked
> > (Psalm 146:7-9).

Why a chapter on loving the poor in a book devoted to evangelism? It goes back to the most basic passage on bearing fruit—John 15. Jesus is clear: Abide in me and you will bear much fruit. As the years of our Christian lives pass by, this should entail more than our morning devotional time. It means becoming like the original vine, having his heart and attitudes. This process will absolutely result in a fruitful and effective life.

God loves the poor. Jesus loves the poor. When we love the poor, it softens us, deepens us, stretches us, breaks us and makes us like Jesus. As we grasp this all-important aspect of Christ's character, we become more effective in our mission to the lost, whether they be materially rich or poor. If evangelism begins in the heart, then in order to bear much evangelistic fruit, that heart must be one that loves the poor.

The fulfillment experienced by loving the poor cannot be matched by materialistic wealth, educational achievements or career advancement. Even the most talented people in society must sit up and take notice when we genuinely love the poor. In Tokyo we often take people who are studying the Bible with us to visit a retirement home or an orphanage. While serving alongside us, these materialistically blessed yet empty-hearted friends often realize what they are missing. They are humbled by learning to love the poor by imitating Jesus, the greatest example in history.

Loving the poor opens the door for the gospel. Minds clouded by drugs must be cleared in order to grasp God's word. Lives lived on the losing edge of survival must be preserved in order to respond to the gospel. Loving the poor never replaces the ultimate, spiritual mission of seeking and saving the lost. However, being loved like Jesus loved is often the first step in a journey that, prayerfully, will end in the kingdom of God.

Now Is the Time

Compassion for the poor must be a hallmark of our present-day movement. The statistics show that while we breathlessly hail the avalanche of technological breakthroughs in medicine, computers and genetics, the worldwide disparity between rich and poor is increasing. Millions, in nations we want to evangelize, live in conditions unimaginable for many of us in the developed world. If we do not become excellent in the grace of giving, if we do not exhibit a powerful, active compassion for the poor, then our hope to reach these lost nations may very well end in disappointment.

You Are the One

You do not need to visit Africa or India to begin. Whether you are standing outside an overcrowded hospital in Phnom Penh or living in an affluent suburb in the US, begin with compassion and willingness. You may not yet know what to do. Open your eyes in compassion, and God will show you the needs. Say, "I am willing," and God will use you to touch someone's life.

Loving the poor means making no excuses. The next time you think that you are too busy to help out at a soup kitchen, tutor an underprivileged child or encourage the elderly, I want you to think of the King Sihanouk Hospital staff. Think of Laurie Felker, RN who moved from LA. Of the Dr. Cameron Gifford family who moved from Boston. Of Dr. Graham Gumley who literally gave up his career as one of the top hand surgeons in the world to move his family to Phnom Penh. For these Christian heroes, loving the poor meant uprooting themselves from comfortable, convenient lives and transplanting their families and futures into the sometimes hostile, always challenging soil of Cambodia. They have already been through civil war, disease and violent crime— and they have counted it a privilege to serve Christ by loving the poor.

The harvest? During the first full year of operation, the King Sihanouk Hospital staff saw over thirty Cambodian health professionals (doctors, nurses and medical technicians) baptized into Christ! These new brothers and sisters, and those who are sure to follow in their footsteps, are already forming a bedrock of faith upon which the Cambodian church will be built. Eternal history is being made.

Your contribution enables them to do their work, which is also our work. Your prayers strengthen them for their task, which is also our task. Your imitation of their compassion and willingness invites God to use all of us as his true church in the ultimate task of evangelizing the world in our generation.

Faith-Building Stories

The Sihanouk Hospital Center of HOPE (SHCH) in Phnom Penh, Cambodia, has received much praise for its work in healing the physical needs of the poor and needy in Cambodia. The number of patients treated and healthcare professionals receiving training and education has steadily climbed since its opening in December of 1996. However, the greatest impact of the SHCH on Cambodia is the salvation of the souls of the patients and staff that it serves. Here are seven such stories.

This story told by Angela Wade, Laboratory Director, SHCH, Phnom Penh, Cambodia:

"But those who suffer he delivers in their suffering;
   he speaks to them in their affliction" (Job 36:15).

When I think of having impact that is a result of serving the poor, I cannot help but think of Dr. David Traver's role in bringing Sokunthea, a sixteen-year-old who was suffering from the later stages of leukemia, to Christ. Sokunthea was brought to the hospital on the advice of her uncle, Dr. Sarim, a disciple and a staff physician at SHCH. Dr. Sarim referred her to Dr. Dave (Traver) and it was not long before Dave diagnosed her with leukemia. Dave immediately sought assistance in prayer from the International Medical ministry of the Phnom Penh Church of Christ. He sought medical assistance from various contacts in the US for her, as well. However, Sokunthea's condition steadily declined. Dave had to tell her and her family that there was nothing more he could do to help her physical condition. But he encouraged her to seek God and introduced her to the sisters in the church. About two weeks later, Sokunthea began to study the Bible and the entire church rejoiced.

It was especially inspiring when Blady and Ceilo Perez, the evangelist and women's ministry leader for the church, shared about Sokunthea while we were having dinner one night. They talked about how she was challenged to confront her family with her intentions to become a disciple. This was a difficult task because of the strong Buddhist traditions that her family followed. Sokunthea met the challenge head on and immediately began to share her faith fervently with her mother, father, two brothers and two sisters. In fact, her mother listened in on the studies. Her love for God was so evident that her family did not try to prevent her from becoming a disciple.

Sokunthea was then baptized into Christ. Her health was declining, but her faith climbed, and even in pain she rejoiced every day as she followed Christ. She always shared kind words and never complained. She was so happy that I really believed that she would overcome death!

But Sokunthea died a peaceful death on a Saturday morning at the SHCH. Her family, out of respect for her convictions, allowed the church to hold a memorial service. Held in a theater, the service had standing room only as schoolmates, hospital staff, disciples and her family celebrated her life and listened to Dr. Dave preach the gospel of salvation. After hearing all of the sharing about Sokunthea and feeling the love in the room, her mother and one of her sisters decided to begin studying the Bible. Her mother has imitated the courage that Sokunthea displayed by facing a learning disability in order to read the Bible her daughter left to her.

Dr. David Traver helped hundreds of children physically as he served HOPE worldwide in Asia. Sokunthea is one patient whose body he could not heal as a doctor. But, as a disciple of Jesus, he helped her to be spiritually healed.

As told by Chiara M. Gifford, Phnom Penh, Cambodia:

When HOPE worldwide sent a medical team to Phnom Penh, Cambodia, to open the Sihanouk Hospital Center of HOPE, the disciples were introduced by Bernie Krisher to an orphanage on the outskirts of the city. Even with the enormous task of opening a hospital ahead of them, the team made a plan to visit the orphanage every weekend to play ball with the children and to look for opportunities to meet some of their needs. Volunteers from the Phnom Penh Church of Christ joined in the outreach to the orphans. One team member donated time every week to teach English to the older orphans and the staff. Later, the HOPE Youth Corps provided playground equipment for the children. At Christmastime a toy drive and a nativity play performed by the children of Phnom Penh disciples were some other outreach activities.

When we first met Saroth he was eighteen years old. His parents had given him and his siblings to the orphanage when he was twelve years old because they could not feed the children or themselves. Saroth worked hard every day to serve at the orphanage where he lived. But he had dreams of moving out of the orphanage and getting a job to support himself. In order to get a job he was studying English every evening on his own from a book. Saroth wanted his life to have meaning, but he did not know how to make a difference.

As HOPE worldwide and the disciples reached out to the children, Saroth began to ask why they took the time to teach English and to play with the children on Sunday afternoons. His experience in the past had always been that people came in to view the orphanage, made a donation and left. He was curious about the desire that the disciples had for a relationship with him. Then he came to church and started studying the Bible. Two months later Saroth became a disciple of Jesus. He is so excited to have a hope and a future.

Now Saroth works full time for HOPE worldwide as a security guard at the hospital's housing for expatriate staff. He is taking continuing education courses in English and voluntarily teaches English to the neighborhood children. Saroth has been fruitful and productive as a disciple and continues to reach out to his younger siblings at the orphanage—and his parents. Perhaps someday they will all be united in Christ.

As told by Laurie Felker, Nursing Director,
SHCH, Phnom Penh, Cambodia:

Hor Dany was thirty-one years old when I first met her. She had come to interview for a nursing position at the Center of HOPE. Dany had been a part-time instructor at the nursing school in Phnom Penh and wanted to improve her clinical nursing skills. We hired Dany to work at the SHCH. With her she brought a learner's heart, a desire to grow and an enthusiastic attitude. She was living with her husband, who was a soldier, and her parents who were older and unable to work. Dany was their primary caregiver. They lived in a very small apartment near one of the local market areas of the city. Before Dany began working at the hospital, her monthly income was under $30 US per month, and her husband earned only a minimum government salary of about $20 US per month.

Dany became ill in October 1997 with recurrent infections that did not respond to antibiotic treatment, so a further investigation was made. Test results revealed that both Dany and her husband were HIV positive and that Dany's health was deteriorating quickly. The day that I counseled both Dany and her husband about their HIV status, I explained to her that medically there was little I could offer her but that if she wanted eternal life, I could help her to know Jesus. I gave her a Bible in Cambodian that day in my office and encouraged her to read about Jesus.

Dany came back to me one week later having read the entire gospel of John and wanting to know more about Jesus and eternal life. I began studying with her and as her health failed her, her thirst for Jesus only grew.

We had to admit Dany to the hospital, for she had developed pneumonia and respiratory distress. Dany continued to study the Bible in bed, building her faith and learning about God while fighting through many physical challenges—like difficult breathing and high fevers. She broke down many walls and fears that people had about HIV, as she bravely faced her unknown future. Her zeal to know God challenged many of her friends and her family. Dany was determined to become a disciple before she died.

I remember one day when I was with her, she looked over to me and asked me, "How do I do this, Laurie? How do I die?" We talked at length about heaven and what it would be like for her. As Dany struggled to breathe, she persevered through a lot of pain to study the Bible. She knew her time was short and becoming a disciple became her goal in life.

Late one night, following a study of the cross, I was privileged by God to baptize Dany into Christ at the hospital. The next day she was all smiles. Dany lived for another four weeks, continuing to share about her relationship with Jesus with her family and her peers at the hospital.

Dany left behind an example of perseverance and letting no excuses get in the way of becoming a disciple. God's love for her allowed her to attain eternal life with him. The impact of her faith, the walls that she broke down by being open about her HIV status, and the drive that she had to become a disciple left a tremendous impact on many lives. Dany is a modern-day hero to me and to many others.

—

As told by Dr. Gillian Hall, SHCH,
Phnom Penh, Cambodia:

As we visited a dying man, lying in a dark, dirty room, buzzing with flies and smelling of stale urine and feces, we got to know Nga and her beautiful little daughter, Srey Lek. They had also been condemned to this room of death for AIDS patients.

At that time, Nga could not even walk, pulling herself along the floor on her knees to try to reach the squalid bathroom. She was pale and suffering with terrible diarrhea. She had fallen victim to the HIV virus that is devastating Cambodia. But for Nga, there was a happy ending!

Literally loved back to life by her new Christian friends, Nga, a twenty-seven-year-old Vietnamese woman, abandoned long ago by the husband who had passed on the killer disease, found a new will to live. She recovered from the diarrhea and soon blossomed as she was nursed back to better health. Nga and Srey Lek returned to their home in a railway slum, but Nga continued studying the Bible and soon made a decision to be baptized into Christ. Her life was transformed, physically and spiritually!

The Christians helped Nga to move to a better home in Phnom Penh city, and for about nine months Nga enjoyed relatively good health, surrounded by the love and concern of her new spiritual family. She was a very special person who changed the lives of all of those who had the privilege to know her. She taught us both the true meaning of being grateful and how to truly love. Many of her neighbors came to church and some are studying the Bible.

Our dear sister has gone to heaven. Srey Lek, also infected with HIV, recovered from a very severe illness (typhoid septacemia and tuberculosis) and is now very happily living with a wonderful Christian family. Only five years old, she prays every day and is not shy in asking the disciples if they have had their quiet times! Her life is sadly destined to be short, but with God it will be a much different and happier one!

As told by Angela Wade:

He raises the poor from the dust
    and lifts the needy from the ash heap;
he seats them with princes,
    with the princes of their people (Psalm 113:7, 8).

For two years, Sokha worked with Syna at a medical clinic in Phnom Penh. She consistently invited Syna to church, and he repeatedly declined her invitations. Sometimes he was even the cause of slander that she received from her coworkers. Syna had his own thoughts about what Christian women were supposed to be, and Sokha did not fit the description.

Syna is one of two men in his family who have survived the infamous Pol Pot regime. His father, brother and one of his seven sisters died. After the Pol Pot regime, he was given the opportunity to leave Cambodia with one of his sisters. But, he chose to stay and care for his mother and lead the rest of his family.

Syna excelled in his studies and has been trained both as a laboratory technician and a medical assistant. His love for the lab compelled him to choose a career as a laboratory technician. His talents and abilities have led to numerous opportunities to study abroad. However, his heart has kept him in Cambodia. As a result of his work at the Thai-Cambodian border and with other laboratories, Syna decided to decline his status as a government worker, risking a steady paycheck, to seek career opportunities that were independent of the government. Eventually, he applied for a position at the SHCH.

Prior to my arrival in Cambodia all of the laboratory applicants had undergone a preliminary screening. Dr. Ferdie Cruz had interviewed some of them and was very excited about Syna. He believed that Syna would not only be a great lab manager but become an awesome disciple as well. As the directing manager of the laboratory, I needed to reinterview all the applicants through the help of an interpreter. My interpreter turned out to be Sokha who continued to encourage me with the idea that Syna was perfect for the job. After three days of interviews with applicants, Syna did not show up, and my faith was challenged.

On the last day, during the last time slot, Sokha telephoned Syna and found out that he was unaware that he needed to come for another interview. I prayed to God to show me clearly what Ferdie and Sokha saw in this man. I also prayed for a sign that Syna was the best choice for the position of assistant lab manager. Syna arrived, speaking great English, and for the first time during the two months that I had been in Cambodia, I could discuss laboratory medicine as if I were speaking to a peer. We immediately bonded, and my heart went out to him after he explained how tired he was: He worked twenty-four hours a day on call, seven days a week. He was ready for a change.

A month later we met and I offered him the job. He accepted but explained that his current employers would be very upset. In fact they were, but after a couple of dinners with Ferdie, they accepted Syna's resignation and he began working for the SHCH. For the first time in years, Syna got a Sunday free from work and attended the Phnom Penh Church of Christ. He immediately started studying the Bible and was baptized into Christ by Ferdie about a month later!

It has been encouraging watching God bless Syna continuously as he puts God first in his life. One of his sisters has become a disciple and another is studying. Syna has skyrocketed professionally, which can be seen as Cambodian and expatriate laboratory professionals seek his assistance. The ease by which the laboratory has been able to bypass the complicated customs clearance processes that are under his supervision are a hallmark of his excellent work, as well.

Because part of my job is to train a Cambodian national to take my position as the laboratory directing manager, I have learned so much more about how serving the poor can mean to become less so that someone else can become more. There are times when I step back and I look at how God has transformed the lab into one of the most modernly equipped and professionally staffed clinical laboratories in the country.

I believe deep in my heart that no victory is more important than the fact that God, through disciples like Syna, will be running the lab for years to come!

Also told by Dr. Gillian Hall,
SHCH, Phnom Penh, Cambodia:

Sa Voeun and So Phy are members of the HIV support group of the Phnom Penh Church of Christ and are now our brother and sister in Christ. One of the most moving baptisms I have ever had the privilege to attend was that of So Phy. The quiet, gentle wife of Sa Voeun, almost overshadowed by the extroverted, jovial character of her husband, So Phy was baptized into Christ early in 1998.

We had known this couple for a long time and everyone knew that Sa Voeun was studying the Bible. He was always there at the support group, eager to share and to crack jokes—he was always the clown! But it was So Phy who really took God's challenges seriously. She realized that only God had the power to save her spiritually and to help her family. She knew that for her husband and for her, both infected with the HIV virus, life was to be short. Therefore, she was baptized into Christ.

She and her family are extremely poor. Some days So Phy works hard all day skinning fish and earns less than one US dollar. But she still uses what money she has to get transport to study the Bible with her friends.

By the river where they live, she has been seen crying out to God in prayer for help. Her family had already been rejected by their neighbors because of the fear of AIDS, but So Phy is not concerned—she has God! So Phy's love for and faith in God and her love for her new brothers and sisters has kept her strong: physically, emotionally and spiritually.

It was incredible to be at her husband's baptism into Christ weeks after hers. He wept as he talked about his gratitude to God for forgiving all of his sins. He could barely stand at that time because he was so sick.

Soon after his baptism we admitted him to the SHCH and started treatment for cryptococcal meningitis. Although still very sick, he is fighting on at the time of this writing.

I am so grateful for Sa Voeun and So Phy, knowing that their example will help others who are sick and poor and without hope to see that God has an answer for their suffering. I am so grateful to know that one day soon, my brother and sister will be in heaven and that their three children who are not infected with HIV will be cared for by their spiritual family.

As told by Dr. Ruth Toothil, surgeon,
SHCH, Phnom Penh, Cambodia:

Sum Chan was seventeen years old when she first came to SHCH. She was a student and came from a poor family that could not afford medical treatment at any of the other hospitals in Phnom Penh. She lived with her grandparents, aunts, uncles, brothers and sisters in Phnom Penh, following the separation of her parents. She had been suffering from a painful swelling of her right knee for more than six months. An X-ray showed that she had a large bony mass, likely to be a cancer. This was confirmed by a biopsy, and Chan went on to have her leg amputated at another hospital (because our operating rooms were not yet open). She came back to see us several times to make sure the wound was healing well and developed great relationships with the doctors and nurses here.

However, four months later Chan returned, obviously unwell and very short of breath. X-rays of her chest revealed that the cancer had spread into her lungs, and it was clear that she did not have long to live. She was admitted to the hospital so we could help ease her difficulty in breathing.

Mala Khun, one of the emergency-room nurses, reached out to Chan and really helped her to understand God's love for her. Chan knew about Jesus from previously attending a Christian church and was excited to study the Bible. Despite great difficulty in breathing and, thus, concentrating, she was baptized into Christ four days before she was transferred to heaven!

As told by Walter Evans, evangelist,
Greater Philadelphia Church of Christ:

Henry Wells, founder of the nationally recognized "One Day at a Time" (ODAAT) program in Philadelphia, a.k.a. "The Rev," has been showing for over fifteen years that there is a way out of the chemical abuse trap of the inner city. The Rev has taken bold steps by fixing up houses throughout the inner city and building a community of those discarded by society. Because these individuals have hit absolute bottom with no other place to turn, they arrive at ODAAT ready to be interviewed and to be put through a "tough love" program to help them break their addiction.

Wanting to begin a benevolent project in connection with HOPE worldwide in their city, the leadership of the Greater Philadelphia Church of Christ began to ask around for help and input, and that's when they became acquainted with ODAAT. The church provided volunteers to work at a nearby medical clinic and collected a special contribution to help ODAAT purchase their own building.

After many months of being around the church and being impressed by the leaders' spiritual lives, the Rev began to study the Bible. Henry began to open up and come to terms with his own need for God, his own need to be set free. After months of wrestling with the Scriptures and his past, the Rev made his decision. He was baptized into Christ and now knows the full joy of walking with his God one day at a time. The church's love for the poor opened the heart of one who already had God's heart for those in need.

About two weeks after Henry made his decision, his son Mel was baptized into Christ and is now a part of the Washington DC church's teen ministry. Then about four weeks later, Henry's wife, Margaret, was baptized into Christ. Currently, Henry serves on the board of HOPE Philadelphia.

Restore the Fallen

In 1988, Hiromi (then) Yazaki was nineteen years old. She was full of ambition and optimism for the future and her life. She was met by a woman named Yukari, an English teacher who came from New York to join the Tokyo mission team. In a matter of weeks, Hiromi was baptized into Christ. She was one of the first people reached by the Tokyo mission team planting.

Months passed. Hiromi grew spiritually and was even hired to be on the staff of the church. Slowly, however, inside her heart Satan was working to take away her faith. Being on staff became a pressure, so she had to step down. Later, leading a Bible discussion group became a burden, and she stepped out of that position. In the end Frank and I asked her to live with us so that she would not fall away. She was a precious sister to us. Before we knew it, however, Hiromi became deceitful and stayed out until late at night. We were afraid for her soul. One morning, she packed up her bags and left our house, departed from God and disappeared out of our lives. Many tears were shed, because she was someone special who had rejected her faith.

Patient Love

Though years passed, several Christians, including me, never stopped keeping in contact. Though letters or cards were often unanswered, there were a few responses from time to time, giving us the hope to persevere.

In 1996, five years after Hiromi had left the Lord, one of the sisters in Tokyo, Chie, invited Hiromi to her wedding. Hiromi wanted to see the wedding but not any of the Christians. It had been years since she had seen any disciples or the church. Hiromi came to the wedding and sat in the back in the balcony. After many years of separation from the fellowship, she was stunned by the growth of the church and of the love of the Christians.

One week later, I called Hiromi to have lunch with her. I was elated when she accepted my invitation. All week I prayed about my meal with her. What should I say? How should I broach the subject of God? Does she have bitter attitudes toward me? What can I do to help her to come back? Does she even want to come back again?

Hiromi came to the meeting place with her new baby. She was no longer the cute, chubby, young nineteen-year-old that I had remembered, but was now a married woman and mother. I will never forget our lunch together....

Imitate Christ's Love

For most of us in the kingdom, there is a "Hiromi" whom we love and who has fallen away. We can never quite forget the friendship or the special moments we shared with that person. Maybe it has been weeks or months or even years, but the memories of that one person or those two or three special buddies never quite disappear. In fact over the years we keep uttering a short prayer for them from time to time with the hope that they will return home to their Father in heaven and repent of their worldly ways. Some of these people have drifted so far and have hardened their hearts so much that we have lost real faith that they will ever come back to the Lord.

> Who shall separate us from the love of Christ? Shall trouble or hardship or persecution or famine or nakedness or danger or sword? As it is written:
>
> > "For your sake we face death all day long;
> > we are considered as sheep to be slaughtered."
>
> No, in all these things we are more than conquerors through him who loved us. For I am convinced that neither death nor life, neither angels nor demons, neither the present nor the future, nor any powers, neither height nor depth, nor anything else in all creation, will be able to separate us from the love of God that is in Christ Jesus our Lord (Romans 8: 35-39).

Even though those precious friends are now in the world, our Lord and Savior Jesus Christ continues to love them. Nothing that they do, no place they may go and no length of time can separate them from Jesus' love. As Christians, we are called to imitate Jesus. We must have the same attitude and heart as Christ if we want to restore the fallen. It will take great patience and intense love to bring back someone who already knows the truth and has rejected it.

That unforgettable lunch with Hiromi began with uncomfortable feelings. I did not know whether to hug her or to bow to her (the Japanese custom) or just say hi. I was immediately drawn to her little baby boy who was only a few months old. Miraculously, within minutes we were in tears apologizing for the hurts from years ago. That became the open door for me to talk about church, God and her faith. An hour and a half later, she actually agreed to come to church again for a visit! Because Hiromi had been close to many other Christians, they also began to initiate with her as well. One sister,

Chikako, had been especially close to her. Chikako and her husband, Masaki, reached out to Hiromi and her husband with an uncompromising love that eventually brought both of them to church. They also built new friendships with other Christians who sacrificed and prayed for them as well.

Teamwork Is Key

Our evangelism is often limited to new contacts. Evangelism includes all lost souls. Of course, we cannot put all of our focus on people who have left the church. We can, however, send a card for Christmas or write a letter from time to time. These little efforts add up in the end. Even a phone call after many months or years might come to fruition through a simple meal or a quick coffee. In any case, we must trust God to work in their hearts. When several Christians continue to love and to give to these people, it will definitely influence them. Moreover, it is through the love of many that the outreach of the church shows that person Christ's love.

> Some men came, bringing to him [Jesus] a paralytic, carried by four of them. Since they could not get him to Jesus because of the crowd, they made an opening in the roof above Jesus and, after digging through it, lowered the mat the paralyzed man was lying on. When Jesus saw their faith, he said to the paralytic, "Son, your sins are forgiven" (Mark 2:3-5).

It was the effort of the four strong men that enabled this paralytic to be carried onto a roof (and eventually through it), brought to Jesus and forgiven of his sins by Jesus. Not only that, but the paralytic was also given full use of his body again through Jesus healing him. In the same way, it will take the strength of more than one Christian to help someone who has left God. Each Christian is essential in showing that lost soul a different perspective of God and of his grace. In the end, it was the teamwork of several Christians that brought Hiromi back to a faith in the Bible, in Jesus and in God.

After several months of studying the Bible together and reconciling with several Christians, Hiromi was ready to re-commit her life to God. During the 1997 Women's Forum in Tokyo, Hiromi and I stood in front of several hundred women. Before all of those women, Hiromi read a letter stating her repentance and desire to be restored to Christ and to his church. I then asked her two very important questions, the same questions she had answered some eight or nine years prior: "Do you believe that Jesus is the Son of God?"

"Yes," she answered.

"What is your good confession?" I asked.

"Jesus is my Lord!" she said in a loud voice.

The sisters shouted out a big, "Amen!"

There were tears and applause from many, including the two of us. I then concluded, "Because of your good confes-sion, I am able to restore you back to the church in the name of the Father and of the Son and of the Holy Spirit. Amen!" Our whole Bible talk ran onto the stage, and we just hugged each other and cried.

> My brothers, if one of you should wander from the truth and someone should bring him back, remember this: Whoever turns a sinner from the error of his way will save him from death and cover over a multitude of sins (James 5:19-20).

At that moment, I believe a multitude of sins were forgiven. I was even able to resolve some feelings in my heart through this victorious experience.

God wants us to go after the lost sheep. Over and over in Israel's history, God reached out his hand to the Israelites in order to bring back the straying chosen. God calls us to do the same. When a person who has rejected the faith comes back, it is a glorious moment!

"What do you think? If a man owns a hundred sheep, and one of them wanders away, will he not leave the ninety-nine on the hills and go to look for the one that wandered off? And if he finds it, I tell you the truth, he is happier about that one sheep than about the ninety-nine that did not wander off. In the same way your Father in heaven is not willing that any of these little ones should be lost" (Matthew 18:12-14).

Since that time, another sister I had studied with several years ago who had fallen away is presently studying the Bible again. Let us be fully committed to loving all the lost—including those who have strayed away from the faith. Let us take time out today to remember that one person—or two people— whom we were close to who have fallen away and take steps to bring them home again to our Lord in heaven. Our Father is not willing that any of these little ones should be lost; let us have the same heart for those who have wandered away.

Faith-Building Stories

Gabe Shepherd was a ministry intern in the Boston church and, as a young leader, had ambitions to become an evangelist. He was raised up quickly into leadership and things appeared to be going great. However, like a seed that grows up quickly and then dies, Gabe left the church. Although he had many natural talents that God had given him, he did not maintain a friendship and closeness with God.

When Gabe left the church, he told his best Christian friend, Joe Silipo, "Whether it takes ten weeks or ten years, I'm not coming back until I see my need for God...but I will be back!" Little did he know what God had in store for him.

Almost immediately, Gabe was asked to run for state senator in Massachusetts, and it appeared that he was doing very well in the race. However, he discovered things that were unethical and withdrew from the upcoming election. The experience was very disappointing, and he moved home to Georgia where he thought life would be better.

However, God's discipline was awaiting him. His brand new car was smashed by a drunk driver; his father had several strokes and nearly died; and he was in a bar fight that resulted in ten stitches in the neck. All this occurred within the first year of leaving his faith. God was trying hard to get his attention.

Gabe went on to become a police detective and eventually a very "hard" person. From time to time disciples would call Gabe from around the world and encourage him. He would politely thank them and tell them that he was not yet ready to return to God. What eventually got through to him? Oddly, it was not the major disasters but the emptiness of his life that caught up to him.

After seven years, Gabe decided to take Joe up on his offer to move to Phoenix where Joe and his wife, Annie, lead the church. Within three days his house was sold! He resigned from the police department, moved to Phoenix and was restored three months later.

Seven years is a long time! Since his restoration, Gabe has gotten married and is once again working on staff for the church. He has changed so quickly and powerfully since his seven years of wandering! His wandering produced in him a deep gratitude for our patient and merciful God—not to mention gratitude for the patience and mercy of disciples who never gave up praying for him and believing that one day he would eventually come to his senses!

The names in this story have been changed.

It began over ten years ago when I was met by a woman at work who invited me to a retreat in New Hampshire. The event was like nothing I had ever seen or experienced before: lots of people smiling, hugging and loving one another. From that day on I continued to go to church, study the Bible and then was baptized into Christ. Life was awesome as a young, married disciple, although at the time my wife, Sandra, was not a disciple. Life became tough as Sandra persecuted the church and me. Later some devoted sisters studied the Bible with her, and she was baptized into Christ. God's dream and my dream came true!

Then I started struggling and my heart became very hard. Soon sin strangled me to the point that I left God. Little did I know that that was the biggest mistake of my life! I was in "no-man's land," where anything goes. I treated Sandra horribly, and I became the persecutor.

About a month later Sandra left God. Things were okay, or so we thought; but sin was killing us. I became an adulterer, and soon left Sandra with our two children to enjoy my sinful life of drugs, alcohol and immorality. My life was a mess, but I was very blind. I came back to Sandra and became very abusive to her physically, emotionally and mentally. My life took a turn for the worse when my cocaine habit became a four- to five-hundred-dollar-a-week nightmare. Later I tried to commit suicide and spent three days in a coma. The doctors later told me that I had taken enough prescription drugs to literally kill a horse. It was a miracle that I was alive!

As I recovered, I became very humble, realizing that God had given me another chance to repent. I started reading my Bible and praying like never before. I remember praying that I would meet a disciple. God answered my prayer, and I was soon brought back to Christ! It took three years, but Sandra has also come back to the kingdom of God. We began dating and have recently gotten engaged! To God be the glory!

Story by Holly McGee of Dallas:

I was recruited to attend Southern Methodist University in Dallas—a school I had not even heard of three weeks before school was to begin. It was one of the top universities in the nation for my major, choosing only thirty students each year, but I was number thirty-one. On the first day I met a guy I fell in love with, and we started dating. Little did I know that he had been baptized as a teen in the church in Atlanta; but when he went to college, he had decided to leave his relationship with God. Although I had grown up being very religious, I quickly developed an immoral relationship with him. His mother, a faithful disciple herself, talked to me occasionally over the phone. She never condemned me or even talked about my obvious sin. She loved me and sent me presents and treated me like her own daughter.

My boyfriend felt challenged and annoyed by how much I talked about God (even dragging him to different churches and trying to convince him to believe in God), but how little of the Bible I put into practice. He remembered everything he had learned in the church as a teen and finally called his mother to ask for the telephone number to the Dallas church.

One day my boyfriend told me that he was convinced that I was not really a Christian because my life did not match what the Bible says. The next day, Sunday, we were picked up by a man whom I was told lived near us, and we drove thirty minutes, passing hundreds of other churches, to a place where my boyfriend told me people really lived out the Bible. I was surprised that in such a big church everyone still knew each other and recognized that I was visiting.

My boyfriend pointed out a woman in the congregation and told me to tell her I wanted to study the Bible. Later, I was so amazed at the clean and sharp "bachelor pad" where we watched the Super Bowl and by how happy the marriage was of the woman who studied the Bible with me. Also, she drove me to the Greyhound station to go home for Christmas vacation. She called and sent cards and made sure that I could hook up with the church in my hometown.

When I came back, my boyfriend and I ended our dating relationship. We both repented and became disciples in the college ministry in the Dallas church. I have since graduated and now am a professional actress in the arts/media ministry there.

Ten years ago in the church in Springfield, Massachusetts, there was a disciple named Tim Pannell who left the Lord after a few years. Throughout his childhood in Springfield, he and his family were good friends with a future disciple named Latonya. Tim and Latonya began a serious dating relationship after he left the church, and they were planning to marry. He sometimes mentioned the church to Latonya, whose heart was moved enough to contact the sisters in Boston, and soon after, they both began to study the Bible.

Moving to Boston, Latonya was happily baptized, but Tim gave up on his faith again. Pressing on, Latonya remained faithful to God and was blessed with a marriage in God's kingdom, still maintaining a healthy friendship with Tim. Three years later, however, Latonya's husband left the church. (Indeed, we are not promised an easy road.) Sadly, Latonya's heart hardened, and hiding her sin, she too left and moved to South Carolina.

Years earlier, while in Springfield, both Latonya and her mother were good friends with two young siblings, Aretha and Alicia, often baby-sitting them as youngsters. Aretha built a friendship with Tim (after he and Latonya had broken up), began dating him, and they planned to marry. Aretha knew nothing of his past experiences in his faith until they began discussing possibly attending a church together. God, knowing their thoughts, put a disciple in their path, also answering Tim's secret prayer that he would be met. God brought them to a service at the Fleet Center in Boston. Aretha later reflected on the memory of Tim's joy in seeing his old friends.

Tim's heart was again determined to persevere for his faith, as he had also persevered in his battle with diabetes. Aretha Sanders, now the mother of her and Tim's child, Alea, was baptized into Christ. Tim pressed on to be restored to the Lord and his church, while his health progressively worsened. Plans were made to announce his return to God to the whole church, but Tim died, at the age of twenty-nine of diabetes, before the meeting took place.

Since his death, Latonya has returned to her faith and has been restored with dreams of helping to plant a church and helping others overcome. Aretha's younger sister was baptized, while Tim's brother, mother and niece have frequently attended church.

As told by Betty Morehead of Boston:

Jill Meyer strolled down my driveway to look at the items displayed in our yard sale to raise money for the special missions contribution. One of the disciples who was helping us spoke with Jill and invited her to church. She came the next day and was eager to study the Bible. Although her military husband was not spiritually minded, he encouraged Jill in her studies because he could see the changes in her, and she was soon baptized into Christ.

With only three months of being around the disciples, Jill moved to Georgia because of her husband's transfer there. She was determined to drive the two hours to services in Atlanta and soon influenced others to go with her. Then when her husband was sent to Germany, they were stationed even further from disciples. Again she persevered, and God provided "local" leaders in the ministry—only an hour and a half away!—whom she had known in Boston.

But worldliness began to creep into Jill's heart, first through her passion for horses, which became her god. The little time she spent with Christians could not overcome the influences around her. As this began to happen, she stopped writing and calling us in the States, and she left God. She divorced her husband in search of fulfillment through finding "the perfect man." After living with a German man, she met a US military man, and they moved in together.

Periodically, I would pray for Jill, but about a year ago, I consistently began to pray, and God prompted her heart to begin to seek him again (within the same month!). Her relationships were unfulfilling, and Jill began to make the more than two-hour drive to worship services in Munich. She broke up with her boyfriend and acquired an interesting job in protocol for the Army, which put her an hour closer to the church. She knew she needed God in her life, but she was not honest about her inner self, so her friendships with the disciples remained superficial.

One summer afternoon, after deciding not to go to the European Mission Conference in Paris, Jill was ready instead to go on a vacation. She went out of her way to meet the disciples to tell them face-to-face that she would not be going to Paris, but instead, a friend convinced her to hop on the bus and go anyway.

Then, despite making some spiritual progress, and even though she felt torn inside, she went on vacation later that summer with her former boyfriend. Jill became pregnant during that trip and truly became urgent in seeking God. She got back in touch with me. We prayed on the phone and began to e-mail back and forth. The disciples in Munich and Berlin poured out their time and hearts for Jill, and she responded. God answered our prayers with a job transfer through the government to the Air Force base near our house in December.

At each step Jill continued to face her fears, pray for clear answers for life issues and for a deep commitment to God and his church. Nine years after she was first met, Jill was restored to the kingdom of God! Then, two months later, Johnathon Walker Graessle was born. All are confident that God has great plans for his life!

Jim Fuda was a forty-seven-year-old registered professional engineer with a national engineering consulting firm. He had two healthy teenage sons, a supportive wife, a beautiful house and a large salary. He had a religious heritage from his family that made him feel like everything was fine spiritually. However, that was all to change as he accepted an invitation to visit a worship service of the Boston Church of Christ. From that first encounter, Jim was blown away by the warmth, sincerity and zeal of the disciples. His wife and two sons visited the service as well, but everything seemed to be moving too fast for them. After studying the Bible for a couple months, Jim was baptized into Christ.

One month later, Jim was promoted to become the Connecticut Regional Office Manager. He needed to relocate immediately. While his family remained in Boston for seven months, Jim focused

on his work and new home and fatally let his newfound commitment to God and the church slip through the cracks. He thought
that he could be a Christian on his own. As he put it, "My pride let
the lion [Satan] devour me," and he left his faith.

Upon the family's arrival in Connecticut, Jim, Nancy, Mike and
John began looking together for a "comfortable church." They visited many assemblies over the next year and a half. However, what
Jim had experienced in the Boston church was always missing. Not
knowing how the family would feel, Jim announced one day that
he was going to the Hartford Church of Christ and hoped that they
would come. To his joy and surprise, they did. It was not long before everyone was studying the Bible.

Jim confessed his sin to his family and the church and was
restored. Then Nancy was baptized into Christ. She had overcome
her fears of driving at night, water and even sharing in front of
crowds in a dramatic way that inspired every disciple! Next, Mike,
a high-school junior, was baptized into Christ as the first male teen-
ager in the teen ministry. Quickly, he was joined by John, his younger
brother. Praise God!

After studying the Bible for three months, Jim Moyer, a young
Navy Seaman aboard the SSN Pargo, was baptized into Christ. The
challenges of weeks and months at sea and away from the church,
combined with the hardening of his heart due to sin, led Jim to fall
away from God.

After his return from a five-month stretch under the ocean,
the disciples in the Groton/New London church made every effort
to bring him back to the Lord. Jim returned merely half-heartedly
and was still giving in to sin. With continued help from the brothers, Jim's heart began to soften. However, at this crucial time,
Jim's submarine was going back out to sea. In the kind of prayer
that is filled with tears and humor, the brothers asked God for the
only resolution they could see: that God in his power would either
break the submarine so that it could not leave the pier, or that he
would break Jim's arm!

Over the next day or so, as Jim and his fellow shipmates were loading supplies onboard the Pargo, they got a little rough and tumble. Jim and a buddy joined in a little game of trading punches while they waited for the next load of supplies. Taking his turn, Jim threw all of his might into a punch, but instead of impacting the ready shoulder of his shipmate, the squeamish friend decided to block it instead. Bone met bone and Jim's wrist broke from the force of impact!

Jim was placed on desk duty and did not go out with the submarine. Filled with incredible faith, the brothers continued to hang in there with him. One night when he couldn't sleep, Jim stayed up all night going over all the studies that had brought him to God so many months before. God's word and the love of the disciples finally changed his heart, and shortly thereafter, Jim was restored to his faith and his God.

Since that time, Jim has become a great servant of the Lord. He has brought many others to Christ and presently is very grateful to God for blessing his steady dating relationship by turning it joyfully into an engagement to be married.

*As told by Joel Ortega, a freshman at the
University of Massachusetts at Lowell:*

My brother, Junior, and I immigrated to Boston on April 29, 1993, from the Dominican Republic. He was fifteen and I was fourteen years old. At that point in time we were looking for some spiritual direction. Everything seemed as if God had a plan for us because Junior met a girl in high school who was the sister of a disciple in the Boston church. Junior and I met him, and then studied the Bible for just two weeks before we made our decisions to become disciples of Jesus.

Junior and I were very blessed by God because we, together with four other teens, started a teen Bible discussion group, which grew to twenty-two disciples in only the first year! Junior was one of the most fruitful disciples in the group.

While God had a plan for Junior and me, on the other hand, Satan had plans to destroy and deceive. Junior played football and basketball and was involved in many different clubs for the summer.

At the beginning he seemed to be doing well with his commitment to God and his involvement with the school, but Satan was stacking him with sports, popularity and girls. Junior started to compromise his commitment for Jesus in order to please his friends. Because Junior was part of a true church that practiced loving one another, he was receiving help from his brothers and sisters. But that was not enough to hold him to his commitment to Jesus. After two and half years, Junior gave in to peer pressure from friends at school and decided to leave God and live a worldly life.

After leaving God, Junior's life was miserable. He left our parents' home and moved to New York City, where he didn't have anyone to care for him. He was involved in drugs, drunkenness, partying, and he dropped out of high school a month before his graduation to continue what he was doing. Not long after that he went to jail a couple of times. While these things were going on with Junior, the family was deeply in pain and in great depression. I personally prayed and cried almost every day for him to come back to God.

I am so thankful that God kept me faithful so Junior would have an example to follow. I know that my brothers and sisters prayed for Junior also. At the end of 1997, God started to move Junior to realize how needy he was without him. Junior started seeing how much God loved him because there were many times when God saved him from a much deeper disaster than what he already had experienced.

The first decision my brother made was to finish his high-school education. Second, he moved back in with the family and apologized. Third, he changed his friends and then got a legal job. Finally, he decided to give his entire life to Jesus Christ once again.

My brother voluntarily repented and came back to God, but praise God for the brothers and sisters who did not forget him and prayed for his return!

Never Give Up

The little girl ran as hard as she could during her race at school on Sports Day. It was her first year in elementary school. As she ran, she could hear her father's voice echoing in her mind: "Never give up." Unfortunately, she was born with a right foot that was extremely pigeon-toed so she tended to trip over her own feet when she ran. That day, she came in fifth place in the race. It was a great disappointment to her. In her mind, however, she was determined to win some day.

It was a joy to see my daughter, Manami, in third grade cross the finish line and take first place! During the race, Manami remembered her father's lesson: Never give up.

Victory often comes to the person who perseveres and never gives up. Just like Manami's father, our Father in heaven teaches us the same lesson of perseverance. Since God is always on our side, he will reward us when we have faith and fight to the end.

Don't Give in to the Devil's Schemes

Do not be deceived: God cannot be mocked. A man reaps what he sows. The one who sows to please his sinful nature, from that nature will reap destruction; the one who sows to please the Spirit, from the Spirit will reap eternal life. Let us not become weary in doing good, for at the proper time we will reap a harvest if we do not give up (Galatians 6:7-9).

There may be some of us who have not been fruitful for years. Others of us were once fruitful but may feel discouraged by the results in recent years. There are others of us who have personal challenges, which limit us from being able to share our faith on a daily basis. Whatever the situation in which we may find ourselves, the lesson is always the same: Never give up.

Listen to some of the evil words that Satan may whisper to us to make us give up on people whom God has placed in our lives:

"Don't push yourself that hard. They probably didn't come on Sunday because they're not open."

"Give up on her. She seems too busy to study the Bible."

"His life seems so together. He's doing fine without God."

"You could never help that person—only one of the evangelists could."

"Don't call her back. She doesn't seem to like you, so stop bothering the woman."

"Be fruitful? You could never do it because of your situation."

Satan does not want us to persevere through the tough times with people. He wants us to take the comfortable road and avoid making the sacrifices which could save someone's soul. Of course, there are times when we need to focus on those who are more open at the moment. Nevertheless, we cannot give up in our faith. The key to overcoming these temptations from the devil is to remember our Lord and Savior Jesus. When he came on this earth to save us, he had to endure much suffering and hardship so that we could be saved:

> Therefore, since we are surrounded by such a great cloud of witnesses, let us throw off everything that hinders and the sin that so easily entangles, and let us run with perseverance the race marked out for us. Let us fix our eyes on Jesus, the author and perfecter of our faith, who for the joy set before him endured the cross, scorning its shame, and sat down at the right hand of the throne of God. Consider him who endured such opposition from sinful men, so that you will not grow weary and lose heart (Hebrews 12:1-3).

It took perseverance on Jesus' part to enable him to die on the cross and win our salvation. He had to fight Satan's temptations and lies just like we do. He, however, did not surrender to the devil's schemes.

Fruitful Despite Personal Trials

Satan tried to hurt a special family in the Tokyo church some years ago when their newborn baby developed digestion problems. It became so severe that we feared for the little boy's life. Hiro and Kyoko Iwanaga named their boy Yuuki which means "spirit of courage." This name was very appropriate for this little baby as he endured considerable hardship during his short life.

Little Yuuki remained hospitalized for many months after his birth. The church fasted for him so that he would survive the different treatments and operations that he underwent. A miracle happened! He withstood all the treatments and was saved from a premature death. However, Yuuki was going to have permanent special needs, because he was deprived of important nutrients during the initial weeks of his life.

The saga did not end here. Yuuki lived in and out of hospitals for the next several years. It was during this time that his parents met Sachiko whose daughter had been born with a rare disease. This disease had caused the little girl, Erina, to be confined to bed and to be dependent on a life-support system. Little Erina could not move her body or mouth. Her only form of communication was done through various expressions of her eyes and one mobile finger, which her mother developed into Erina's unique language. Erina's mother, Sachiko, and Yuuki's mother, Kyoko, became immediate friends as they suffered together, watching their children go through so many trials.

Little Yuuki was three years old when his mother met Sachiko. Sachiko was impressed by Kyoko's faith and was baptized into Christ several months later. Shortly after Sachiko's baptism, Yuuki contracted sickness after sickness. He seemed to recover one week only to be hospitalized the next. Over a period of months, he fought to survive. God, however, decided to free Yuuki from his suffering on this earth. In 1995, Yuuki went to heaven to be with our heavenly Father. The cause of his death was unknown to the doctor. His little heart just stopped beating one afternoon after a slow deterioration over a period of several weeks.

His father and mother lovingly caressed their son one last time. As they held him, tears poured from their eyes. They kept repeating to Yuuki, "I love you; I love you," over and over again. Then they turned to all of us who were there to support Yuuki. Hiro, Yuuki's father, pulled everyone together and thanked us for our help and love. Then he prayed for strength and praised God for the victories in Yuuki's life. Because of Yuuki, Sachiko was saved. His life and disabilities had resulted in eternal life for Sachiko.

Many times Hiro and Kyoko felt that they were being unproductive and useless in the kingdom. They, however, decided that God was in control and trusted him to guide them through the hard times, as they continued to reach out to the doctors and nurses that helped them. They were also able to share with many other parents who had no support group to help them through the emotions of having a special-needs child. Hiro and Kyoko's determination to fight through the obstacles enabled them to see triumph in their lives. In the words of Jesus,

> "But the seed on good soil stands for those with a noble and good heart, who hear the word, retain it, and by persevering produce a crop" (Luke 8:15).

Personal Challenges Are No Excuse

Sachiko was inspired and spiritually challenged by the Iwanaga's faith in God. She knew that her daughter, Erina, had the possibility of meeting death at an early age as well. Many times Erina had bouts with illnesses that caused her to be hospitalized. Sachiko, however, fought through the difficulties and kept growing in her faith.

Erina is now ten years old. Though she cannot walk or speak, she is growing spiritually and praying for the different nurses and volunteers around her. Sachiko is determined to help her daughter to understand spiritual concepts. Together in the last six months, mother and daughter have helped Erina's grandmother, two nurses and a volunteer for the physically challenged be baptized into Christ! Presently, Erina's great-grandmother is also studying the Bible because she has seen all the amazing changes in the lives of her family.

Sachiko's and Erina's joy and love for God have brought many people to church. For them there are no excuses for not being joyful and thankful in the Lord. In fact, when Sachiko asked her daughter if she felt badly that she could not move or walk, Erina just answered in her specially developed language, "Mom, I do walk. When you push me in my wheelchair, I am walking. I also run, because when you push me fast, I am running."

There is no excuse for us not to give to others the joy and the love of Christ. No matter what situation we are in, we can meet and share our faith with people. Though we may not be able to personally study the Bible with them, we can tell them how Jesus changed our lives and invite them to church. Then other Christians can study with them.

It is when we overcome trials and challenges that God is glorified. Through the Iwanaga's little boy, Yuuki, God was praised and glorified. During his five years on this earth, he never spoke, stood up or walked. In heaven, however, Yuuki is speaking with God, standing before his throne and dancing with the angels. I am grateful to his parents who persevered and remained faithful. Through Yuuki and his family dozens and dozens of people are now saved for eternity.

> "Which is easier: to say to the paralytic, 'Your sins are forgiven,' or to say, 'Get up, take your mat and walk'? But that you may know that the Son of Man has authority on earth to forgive sins...." He said to the paralytic, "I tell you, get up, take your mat and go home." He got up, took his mat and walked out in full view of them all. This amazed everyone and they praised God, saying, "We have never seen anything like this!" (Mark 2:9-12).

Let us look at our physically challenging situations or years of fruitlessness with a new attitude. Let us look at the obstacles that are blocking us from believing that we can be fruitful, and let us overcome those hindrances by faith. Anyone can produce fruit! Let us renew our vision and remember that there is someone waiting for us to touch their lives just like Hiro and Kyoko influenced Sachiko—and many others.

Look at your situation objectively and honestly. Even if your only obstacle is time or a lack of faith, God can make miracles happen. Being honest and open is the beginning of resolving your problems. Have you really been making the most of every opportunity? Have you just stopped preaching God's word because you have convinced yourself that you have no time? Challenge yourself to do something radical today. Even as I wrote this chapter, I challenged myself and the four women region leaders of the Tokyo church to collectively share with a thousand people in seven days. I have a new-born baby and two of the women are seven months pregnant! What will you do today? Open your eyes to the harvest and remember your heavenly Father's words: Never give up!!

Trust in God's Timing

Never giving up applies to another area as well. Sometimes the people we reach out to do not respond quickly. Sometimes they do not appear to be open at all, but many are disciples today in the kingdom of God because someone refused to give up on them. Sharing your faith and making disciples requires a great deal of hard work. It is like having and raising children. There will be ups and downs. There will be moments of elation and moments of disappointment. But disciples who never give up on what God can do through them and disciples who never give up on what God can do in others will live to see and to celebrate the fruits of their efforts. They will be overjoyed to welcome someone who has become a very best friend into the fellowship!

Whether the temporary lack of results seems to come from our own circumstances or someone's unresponsive heart, we must stay focused on the mission, never stop loving people and never stop trusting that God will bring a harvest.

Faith-Building Stories

Nicha Thompson, a disciple in the arts and entertainment ministry in Atlanta, met Speech and Yolanda Thomas while working as a backup singer in Speech's band, Arrested Development. Initially, Speech was not open to coming, although he was familiar with the church, having been invited five other times by five different disciples. In addition, several years earlier, before his group became nationally known, Speech stayed with some Christians in the New

York City church while doing a show there. This was arranged by Tia Scott, a disciple in the arts ministry there and an old friend of the Thomas family from Milwaukee. She had been inviting Speech to come to church since she had become a Christian.

Speech and Yolanda finally made it to church and agreed to study the Bible immediately after that first visit. They both fell in love with the word of God, sensing that it was what they needed and had been looking for in their lives. Despite being on tour with Hootie and the Blowfish throughout the Northwest and Canada, they both continued to study the Bible as they traveled.

Speech was continually amazed at the disciples who came out to see Nicha, who was on the tour with Arrested Development. In every city a group would come out to support her, even though they did not know her! He marveled at how much disciples loved one another. When they returned to Atlanta, they were very urgent to finish studying and be baptized into Christ. On that exciting day, they had forty-two friends and family members there to witness it. Since that time they have seen Yolanda's mother and father, some dear friends from Milwaukee, a musician Speech works with and a business associate all baptized into Christ!

It took at least six disciples and six different invitations, but two people finally became disciples, and since that time the fruit has multiplied.

As told by Emmanuel Umesi:

Moving to Boston to seek more education after college, I quickly got a temporary job with the Yankee Bank. A disciple worked at this bank, and she invited me to a worship service at the Boston Garden on Sunday. There was a huge crowd, and they were hugging each other, whether white, black or whatever color. I never found the woman who invited me, but I decided to revive my spiritual life.

I went home and called the woman who invited me, and she told me about a midweek Bible discussion group, where she introduced me to a fellow Nigerian, Babatunde (Babs). We set up a time to study the Bible, but my heart was not open to the studies or to the changes I needed to make. We stopped studying, but Babs became my closest friend. Once in a while he tried to persuade me to study the Bible or to come to church.

Babs got married, and he and his wife had a baby. Meanwhile, my girlfriend was pregnant with our son. Two weeks after our baby was born, my girlfriend and I started having all kinds of domestic problems. Babs invited me to church again, but I refused. Instead, I would work double shifts on Sunday to pay rent and support the family. Everything seemed so hard; nothing went smoothly. Eventually, I left my home, my wife and my son.

I remember calling Babs from a homeless shelter one Saturday evening. In less than one hour, he was there. We cried and prayed together. He took me to his house, and we prayed and went to church together the next day. By this time I was dependent on chemical substances to function and was unable to study the Bible. The only clothes I had were the ones I had from before my hard times or ones I collected from charities.

Babs continued being my friend. Anytime we met, he would support me. He would remind me of my dreams: graduate school, family and friends. I had shut myself off from everyone. Babs showed me patience, perseverance and love. About eight or nine years had passed since I had first met him. I had lost everything: two cars, my home, all my personal belongings, my wife and my son.

After two years of being sober, I started looking for Babs. He had moved, and the only way I knew to find him was to go back to the Boston Garden. I went every Sunday until there was a worship service there. Finally there was one, but I did not find Babs in the multitude. I met someone who knew him, gave her my phone number and asked her to give it to Babs. He called and as usual, his first question was, "Where are you?" I told him, and it took him forty-five minutes to come over to my place. I went to church that Sunday. After about ten years of running, I finally opened my heart to the word of God and was baptized into Christ! I have been a disciple for four years now, and God even brought my son back to me: He is ten years old now, and I miraculously discovered that he lives on the next street over from me.

With a heart full of love and dedication, I thank Babatunde and his family, who stayed there for me throughout my period of turmoil.

Mark Braunlich has led an exciting and diverse life. He won a full academic scholarship to the University of Pennsylvania. There he won the honor of Most Outstanding Chemistry Student, and earned a starting position on the freshman wrestling team. He left UOP after two years and moved to California to work in the High Sierra mountains: first as a US Forest Service trail-crew member and firefighter, then as a Wilderness Ranger. Nearly ten years later, he resumed academic studies at the University of California, Davis, earning an economics degree with honors and a teaching credential in mathematics two years later. Mark worked as a mountaineering guide, a white-water guide and as Director of Outdoor Adventures for UC Davis. He also piloted a high-school physics program for the California State Department of Education for two years.

After the death of his stepfather, whom he had helped care for, Mark ran in the Moscow marathon and explored Europe for several weeks. Returning to California, he decided to sell everything and move to the Netherlands. One morning while ordering coffee in a Davis cafe, he heard an employee telling a joke with a heavy Dutch accent. Rico, the employee, was skeptical about talking to him since he had no work permit and thought Mark was an immigration agent! Nonetheless, Rico helped Mark study Dutch, and they became good friends. A couple months later, Mark flew to Holland, and Rico continued his world travels, during which time he was baptized into Christ in the Sydney church. Later, Rico was on the mission team to plant the church in Amsterdam from London.

Mark, meanwhile, was busy running a Dutch industrial public relations firm that called him to work frequently between Holland and Russia. He was one of the four Americans who ran the first International Siberian Marathon, and he set up a US/Dutch non-profit organization which trained European and Russian secondary school teachers in global computer network communication.

Years later Mark's glamorous lifestyle went into a downward spiral. One summer he left his girlfriend behind in Moscow to work in Europe and to see his mother who was then visiting Amsterdam. A friend met him at the airport with the news that his mother was hospitalized. The following day Mark was with his mom as she received the diagnosis of terminal cancer.

Mark returned with his mother to her home in California and cared for her until her death five months later. During this time Mark arranged for his Russian girlfriend to visit California. He wanted her to meet his mother before she died. He hoped they would soon be married. She ended up leaving him at the end of her visit, and back in Moscow she aborted their child.

Following his mother's death, Mark made several trips to Moscow. Passing through Amsterdam on one trip, Mark was violently attacked by two men with knives. One held a knife to his throat and the other sliced his coat and his hand. At that moment he understood he was not prepared for his own death.

Arriving back in the States, Mark was severely shaken emotionally. He had spent the previous five years logging onto the Internet at least ten times daily; now he could not bring himself to physically touch his computer. In search of inner peace, he spent the summer studying Buddhism and meditating.

Then Mark returned to Amsterdam to get away and to be alone. On one of his lowest days, he walked down the street to a neighborhood store. God placed him in the same aisle as his friend Rico, who had been praying for Mark since he had become a disciple. Though they had kept in touch, they had only seen each other a handful of times in the intervening years. Rico encouraged Mark to visit the church, and after weeks of hesitation, Mark went. He was moved and began studying the Bible. He started out not believing in God at all—a complete atheist! He did much reading outside of the Bible, attended all church meetings and studied consistently, but became stuck: There were no older men in the church (he was forty-three at the time) and no resources that dealt with faith and science.

Mark returned to California a few months later to continue his Bible studies in the Sacramento church and to sell his mother's home. There he found Scott Leeder, an older, married disciple with a civil engineering degree. With Scott he further studied the Bible and worked through science issues. He found books that dealt with evolution and the Bible. Finally, as Mark puts it, "My doubts were worn down. At every point where I challenged the Bible, the Bible won," and he was then baptized into Christ!

Mark describes his turning point: "After looking at the evidence, I concluded it is more logical than not to believe in a Creator. The existence of a Creator implies absolute truth. Seeing the logic of absoluteness opened my heart and mind to study the God of the Bible, and to start making changes in my life. I realized that if God exists, it was better for me to search out his truths than to indulge in my own opinions."

Mark believes deeply in Jesus and states, "I can't avoid that Jesus is the truth; the more I tested, the truer he became." Mark is now a part of the great Los Angeles church.

—⋘

As told by Amy Jones of Boston:

When I was a college student, I was hired by a nonprofit agency for a three month internship. Despite the fact that I really didn't know too many people, for some reason I decided to go to the Christmas party there. I ended up singing a karaoke song. On my way out the door, a young, attractive woman introduced herself, telling me her name was Danae and that she loved my singing. As we talked, I found out that she was on a date with one of the employees. I shared with her about church, and she told me that she had tried a lot of different religions and was not satisfied.

Whenever I called her on the phone after that, we would have long talks. I would share scriptures with her that I thought might help her in some of the things she was going through. Finally, after about six months of saying she wanted to, she came to a Sunday worship service. She wept through it. Afterward, at lunch, Danae opened up about her life and told my friend and me that she was a prostitute. She also told us about the drugs that she had done and how it was hard to be different because of the people she was surrounded by. Later that day when I saw the people in her living room smoking pot, I told her that she could stay with me if she needed to just get away from that scene.

The next Saturday was Woman's Day, which she had wanted to attend, but she did not show up. I called her from there but just got the answering machine. After leaving messages for a few weeks, I discovered that her phone number was out of service because she had moved.

Almost two years later I was in Europe going through a difficult time spiritually. On one of my worst days, I had a conversation with my mom, who is a disciple. She told me that someone I had met had become a Christian—Danae—but I could not believe it. That news lifted my spirit!

When I returned to the States and saw Danae, I did not even recognize her; she was a new woman! We hugged and cried, and she told me the story. She had had a terrible nightmare about spiritual things and was very shaken up. The next day at work, a man who had once been a disciple showed up at the hospital where she worked. She had not seen him since the day she had come to church with me. She told him that she had to go back to church, and he told her where they were meeting. She went and later began studying the Bible. When she decided to tell her boyfriend she wanted to break up with him because of her newfound convictions, he ended up holding her hostage in a hotel room. He had his hands around her neck, intending to strangle her, and all she could say was, "God." Amazingly, he let go, and she was able to escape. Four weeks later she was baptized into Christ!

This year it was an amazing privilege to watch Danae marry a spiritual man who loves her with all of his heart. Together they lead a group of disciples in the Boston church. She has met several women in the past few years who have become Christians.

Raised in atheistic Germany, Thomas Nolte was living his dream of being a jet pilot in the Air Force when severe arthritis in both knees forced him into early retirement. His twenty-four-hour-a-day goal then became earning enough money in the next few years to be able to retire for good. Having achieved his goal, he still wasn't happy, so he decided to travel the world. He moved to San Diego to live on a sailboat, enjoying trips to Alaska and to Hawaii, where he met Gillian.

Gillian was born in England into a family in which God was only really talked about on Sundays. Her dreams of love, purity, raising a family and "living happily ever after" faded quickly as she pursued her career and relationships with men. After ending an abusive relationship, she went with a new boyfriend to New Zealand. This relationship lasted only a few weeks, and she ended up enjoying a six-month stint as a nanny there. Returning to England after her visa expired, she intended to earn money to travel again. Her first stop was Hawaii where she met Thomas and decided to stay with him. They then went to live together in California but broke up a few months later, and she returned home.

One Sunday, just after Gillian had left, Thomas saw a large group of people in a park. Thinking it was a music concert, he walked over and found that it was a worship service of the San Diego Church of Christ. He stayed, and seeing their relationships and their joy, he asked to study the Bible. Realizing that he didn't really want to be a disciple, he stopped studying and flew to see Gillian on her birthday. Sharing what he had learned about godly relationships, they decided to get married a few months later in a denominational church.

During that time Gillian's mother was diagnosed with terminal cancer, so she and Thomas took care of her until her death. Then, because of Thomas' health, they moved back to San Diego. They visited churches but found mainly hypocrisy and emptiness. One day they walked past a sign that read "The San Diego Church of Christ meets here." Since this was the church Thomas had attended before, they decided to go the next Sunday. With mixed emotions, they attended. Thomas was not at all sure that he wanted to be there. During the service Gillian was amazed at the love she saw, and she knew that she wanted what they had.

Thomas recognized Joe Fields with whom he had studied the Bible in the previous year, and Joe invited them to his house for dinner the next week to meet his family. They shared their lives and faith with Thomas and Gillian, and they began to study the Bible. Two weeks later, they were both baptized into Christ. Ten months later they moved back to Germany to be with the church there.

Today they live in Berlin and have set up HOPE Germany, a benevolent nonprofit organization that cares for the elderly in the cities. The first senior center under HOPE worldwide, a daytime facility for seniors, opened its doors in Berlin last fall.

Bill and Sandy Stahlke of Atlanta were self-made millionaires, and Bill had retired at the age thirty-five. Outwardly, they lived a glamorous lifestyle filled with travel, golf and shopping. However, they were having trouble in their marriage and with their two young children. Eric and Lynn Triebold were at a Dairy Queen, and the Stahlkes were the only other people there. Wanting to share their faith, the Triebolds felt it was clear that God was setting up this golden opportunity to invite this family to church.

The Stahlkes came to church a few times over several months, and eventually Sandy began to study the Bible. She became a disciple many months after that first meeting at Dairy Queen. Bill, however, was not ready to explore Christianity for almost another year. Finally, because of what he saw in his wife and the way the other disciples continued to reach out to him, he saw his need for God, studied the Bible and was baptized into Christ! Their marriage is getting better and better, and they are learning how to Biblically raise their children. They recently started leading a Bible discussion group.

As told by Kim Phipps of Los Angeles:

As a senior journalism major at the University of Texas, I had the privilege of attending the Sorbonne, a prestigious university in Paris, for a year. During that time, I met a French woman in the metro, and we exchanged numbers. She did not invite me to church right away, and I am glad she did not at the time. Having grown up in the Bible belt in the US, the last thing I ever wanted to be a part of was a religious group.

However, my father's unexpected death the year before had left me searching for answers to life's more spiritual questions. Two months after we had met, I decided to call the woman from the metro who had been so kind to me for no apparent reason. It turned out that she had been trying to find me, but I had moved without leaving a forwarding number. She invited me for dinner, where she first shared her faith with me. This surprised me, because most of the French students I knew seemed to be atheists or agnostics with a few denominational ones thrown in. But this woman and her friends seemed to be very sincere in their faith, and I was amazed at their Bible knowledge, considering most of my religious friends back home did not seem to know half as much as they did!

I was curious, but cynical, and went to church on and off for six months, trying to find out what was "really going on" with these people. After running out of excuses, I finally agreed to study the Bible with Adrienne Scanlon, who led the campus ministry women at the time. I was very close to making my decision to be a disciple when I realized that a *big* challenge was facing me: Since there was no church of disciples in Texas at the time, I had to choose between moving back to Austin to finish my degree and staying in Paris and becoming a disciple. My college education had always been my idol, so I told the disciples that I simply could not give it up—for anything.

I said good-bye and booked my one-way nonrefundable ticket back to Texas. I was determined not to give in to my conscience, which constantly told me that I needed to stay there and get right with God. The day before my plane left, I called to reserve a cab for 5:00 am the next day in order to make my flight. But I could not sleep that night; I was so confused and couldn't decide what to do. So, one hour before I was supposed to leave forever, I asked God to show me in one hour what I needed to do. I opened my Bible and started reading. It took about ten minutes in God's word to show me that everything in the world that I was putting my confidence in could be taken away: my career, my degree, my family, all of it.

So, that morning I ran over to the Scanlon's house—at about 5:00 am!—and begged them to let me know whatever I had to do in order to become a Christian, no matter what cost I had to count. They were quite surprised to see me! They did just that, and I was baptized into Christ three days later!

And God was faithful. Everything that I thought I was giving up, God gave back to me. I eventually did move to New York for school, and then to Texas (once there was a church of disciples there, of course) where I graduated and even went on to further studies. Two years ago, God blessed me even more by allowing me to move to LA, and giving me a great career in the film industry.

—————

As told by K. Michael Bibalo:

Linda and I met in Freemantel, Australia. I thought I was a Christian, and Linda believed in God but was not a churchgoer. When I returned to the US, we kept in touch for about five months. I was praying that if it was God's will, Linda would come to the US so we could see what would happen with our relationship. She arrived here, and we were married a month later!

When we returned from our honeymoon, Linda had to get a physical examination, which was the beginning of the immigration process. The doctor found a lump on Linda's neck, and we later found out that the lump was cancerous. She was operated on and was recovering when we got a call telling us that the cancer she had was very rare; she needed a second operation as soon as possible. According to the doctors, this fourteen-hour operation would be the only way to effectively remove all the cancer.

During all this Linda and I tried very hard to trust in God. We prayed and read the Bible a lot. We put our hope in Proverbs 3:5-6. The first year of our marriage was spent in physical therapy and other follow-up doctor's appointments.

I changed jobs, which brought us to Groton, Connecticut. After being there for nearly a year, Linda and I were invited by Ryan Black to attend the Groton/New London Church of Christ. At that time we were attending a denominational church and leading a small teen group. Within that church, however, we saw the lack of unity, lack of spirituality and a real lack of love. We were searching for a true relationship with God, but what we were becoming was religious.

After months of his invitations, we agreed to go with Ryan to a large worship service held at an outdoor performing-arts center in Massachusetts. When we left the service, we both agreed that this was the church for us. We were both so inspired by the love that everyone had for one another! We both started to study the Bible. Then I was baptized into Christ, and two weeks later Linda was baptized into Christ. (Also, Linda no longer has a trace of cancer left in her, praise God!)

A few months later Linda invited my sister Sherrie to a Women's Day. Sherrie traveled from Pennsylvania to attend, and she had a great time. Her daughter, Carrie, also visited and attended a Bible Jubilee. Sherrie decided to move with her fifteen-year-old son, Rich, to be part of the Groton church. Carrie had been one week away from joining the Army when God intervened in her plans, so she also moved to Connecticut. She started studying the Bible and was baptized into Christ that same month! Meanwhile, Rich was also studying and was baptized into Christ two weeks later. Then Sherrie was baptized into Christ a week later!

All the praise, of course, goes to God for how he orchestrates our lives so that we may have a relationship with him!

As told by Denis DuMaine:

I had been sent to Chicago by my medical faculty in Paris to carry out some additional research at the University of Illinois at Chicago on the working of the brain. Exactly two days after my arrival I was riding on the subway on my way to meet a girl when a young man started talking to me. His name was Ruben, and as we chatted for half an hour, we really hit it off and ended up exchanging phone numbers. He called me consistently for the next three weeks inviting me to all kinds of activities and eventually to church. Because we had become such good friends I accepted, and sure enough, he came banging on my door every Sunday after that, waking me up and driving me to church.

Every time I attended, I was deeply touched by the warmth and feeling of fulfillment that emanated from all these Christians, and I started to study the Bible to try to understand where all this came from. But my heart was not with it—only my head—and I soon gave up studying.

Still, Ruben stayed faithful in his friendship, as did many other disciples in Chicago, and when the time finally came for me to fly back to Paris, he accompanied me to the airport. There he told me that he had the faith that I would become a Christian soon and that I would eventually lead a church somewhere in the world. I didn't take him seriously and once more proclaimed that this life was not for me, although I was very touched by his friendship.

I went back to France, and for the first two months the brothers and sisters from Chicago tirelessly called me and wrote to me every week to ask me how I was doing and to encourage me to go to church. Eventually, one brother asked me to go at least once to take pictures of the church and send them back to him (a clever ploy!). I accepted, and when I arrived that morning, I was struck once more by the atmosphere and the power of the message. I met Thierry Fender, and he too persevered for two months before I finally started studying the Bible again. At last I was baptized into Christ, nine months after I had first been met by Ruben on the Chicago subway. And, true to his prediction, I am now the evangelist of the Brussels Church of Christ in Belgium, which I lead with my wife, Eléonore (another story of perseverance!). We have recently been blessed with the birth of our baby girl, Lea.

Epilogue

I've got to be honest. Writing this book was not my idea. In fact I spent several weeks trying to think of "legitimate" reasons for politely declining! Not that I think that a book on evangelism isn't important. To Erica and me, it's indisputable: The mission of the church and of every disciple of Christ is to seek and save the lost. This was precisely what made me hesitant—the supreme and ultimate importance of the subject. We have moved our family literally around the world to make disciples of all nations but are still far from being what we should be in terms of our passion and zeal for the mission. Paul's words both inspire us and haunt us:

> "I consider my life worth nothing to me, if only I may finish the race and complete the task...of testifying to the gospel of God's grace" (Acts 20:24).

Every time I read or preach these words, I am set afire by the purpose God has given me. I am also quite humbled by how far I still have to go, thus the reluctance to sound like a final authority on the topic.

What's amazing to me is that after all these years, when the stakes are high and a friend is on the brink of deciding to follow Christ, it always comes down to the same battle. It always requires humbly pouring out my heart. It always demands loving beyond the fear of rejection. It often calls for tears. Above all else, it always takes a miracle from God. There is no guaranteed technique, and it's never neat and easy. I guess that shouldn't surprise me. It wasn't neat and easy for Jesus or any of his men.

This much I do know: I am devoting the rest of my life to getting there. We can't level off thinking that we have "figured it out." We can't fit evangelism so comfortably into our lifestyle that it's not a strain anymore. (What a deceitful ploy of Satan!) To be quite honest, my life in Christ has evolved into a continual struggle to keep my focus clear and simple: to always strive to bring more souls back to God. That fight has intensified proportionally to the number of responsibilities and roles that life has given me. When I see Paul, already imprisoned for preaching the Word, praying in his cell to speak even more fearlessly, I realize that this will be a fight for the rest of my life. At the same time, what a glorious battle! What purpose could ever be more meaningful? What struggle could ever result in a better, more glorious crown than the continuing effort to impact more and more souls for eternity?

After reading this book, please accept this challenge. Get on your knees. What does God want you to do? There is no ambiguity here. God's will is absolutely clear. He wants his children saved. Do you feel the desperate heart of God? Can you say, "I count my life worth nothing to me if only I may finish the race and complete the task of testifying to the gospel of God's grace?" Decide to get there, even if it takes a lifetime!

After you've prayed, get up and…go! Now! Hopefully you've figured out that the fields are ripe for the harvest. Simply reading this book won't change a single soul's eternity, and it doesn't make you more effective or more spiritual. It's what you do now that counts. I know. Writing this book has encouraged and challenged Erica and me! But that alone hasn't saved anyone. We must get up and go in order to get that job done. See you in the harvest field!

Be Still, My Soul

A Practical Guide to a
Deeper Relationship with God

BY SAM LAING

In twenty-two short but poignant chapters, Sam Laing shows how we can all walk with God, enjoy God and have an intimate fellowship with him that gets better with the passing of time. Sharing from his life, from his heart and from the Scriptures, the author shows us the essence of the spiritual life. Here is a book you will return to again and again when your own soul yearns for God.

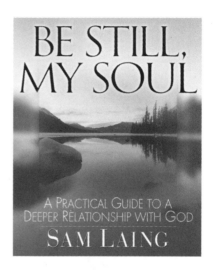

Be Still, My Soul
Music to quiet the soul and inspire the heart

When Kevin Darby and the Triangle Church learned that Sam Laing was writing his book on developing a great relationship with God, there was immediate interest in producing music that would be a great companion to the book. This recording, available both on cassette and CD, will reach your inmost being. It includes both new music and unique arrangements of classics like "Be Still My Soul," "Blessed Assurance," "I Know That My Redeemer Lives," "Where You There?" and seven others.

Quiet Time Journal

In his book Sam recommends that every disciple keep a journal of his or her times with God. This beautiful journal, with the art work from the cover of *Be Still, My Soul,* more than meets the need.

The Promises of God

Edited by Thomas and Sheila Jones

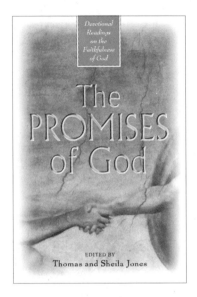

The Bible is filled with what Peter calls "great and precious promises" from God. In this book, leaders from around the world examine some of these promises and show how trusting in them gives strength, confidence and calm to our hearts and minds. God has given us his promises to encourage us and give us a reason to never ever give up. This book will give loads of encouragement to those who read it. As you will read in the opening chapter:

Nothing is more at the heart of this book than this idea: God fulfills his promises—every last one of them. The last man you voted for may not have done a very good job doing what he promised, but God is not like that man or like any man. He is trustworthy, reliable and absolutely faithful to every promise he makes. And since he is God, he has the power to do what he has promised to do. A promise from God is as good as a fact. You can rely on it. You can build on it. You can act on it. You can stand on it.

Letters to New Disciples

BY THOMAS A. JONES

In this book, DPI's editor-in-chief addresses twenty-four vital issues faced by new Christians and helps them see God's plan for winning the battles. The most difficult time for new Christians is in their first few months as a disciple. This book is designed to help them through those early challenges.

The Spirit
The Work of the Holy Spirit in the Lives of Disciples

BY DOUGLAS JACOBY

The Spirit is really two books in one. In Part One Douglas shows in practical ways how to walk in the Spirit and live in the Spirit's power. In Part Two the reader will find a more technical discussion of many issues connected with the Charismatic and Neopentecostal movements of the twentieth century, as well as Biblical answers to a host of other questions. For all of those who want a sound understanding of the living water that Jesus promised (John 7:38), this book will meet many needs.

The Killer Within
An African Look at Disease, Sin and Keeping Yourself Saved

BY MIKE TALIAFERRO

What do the Ebola virus, cholera, meningitis and the Guinea worm have to do with sin? In this poignant book you will find out. Mike Taliaferro has done it again! In his unique style he uses the physical world to paint a vivid picture of the deeper, more crucial issue of sin's effect on the soul. Powerful images of disease and sickness drive home the conviction that sin must never be taken lightly.

The Leader's Resource Handbook, Volume One

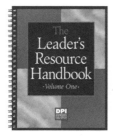

A unique collection of materials from a variety of leaders in one handy volume. This material will train, equip, inspire and motivate. Great for those leading small groups as well as for full-time leaders of larger ministries. Spiral-bound.

Mind Change
The Overcomer's Handbook
(Second Edition–Revised and Expanded)

BY THOMAS A. JONES

Life is full of challenges: pain, illness, insecurity, sin, confusion and death. None of these surprise God. This book is written to help you see (1) your challenges are not unusual and (2) God's plan for overcoming will work for you. Thomas Jones writes out of his experience of living with multiple sclerosis and applies what he has learned to overcoming various challenges.

This Doesn't Feel Like Love
Trusting God When Bad Things Happen

BY ROGER AND MARCIA LAMB

What one family learned as trial after trial, including numerous bouts with cancer, came their way. With refreshing candor the authors share their struggles and victories, their strengths and weaknesses. They show that even when your life is upside down and your emotions inside out, God is still at work, when you hold on to your faith.

Friends and Lovers
Marriage As God Designed It

BY SAM AND GERI LAING

Best friends. Exciting lovers. Rarely has the heart and soul of marriage been summed up any better. Friendship and romantic love are the two essential ingredients of a great marriage, the qualities that will make it grow ever richer, deeper and more fulfilling. Many have seen marriage as a drain rather than a fountainhead, a battleground instead of a refuge, and a pit stop rather than a permanent home. This book shows how all that can change.

Raising Awesome Kids in Troubled Times

BY SAM AND GERI LAING

The Laings provide answers, and they have a family that reflects these principles! Learn to build a solid, happy family using the standard of God's word.

Walking with God

BY RUSS EWELL

Russ Ewell, one of the most dynamic speakers in the kingdom of God, shows that a relationship with God is the most exciting thing a human being can do with his life. Topics include (1) Wrestling with God, (2) Walking with God and (3) One Holy Passion. A DPI best-seller. 3-cassette series.

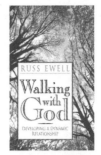

After God's Own Heart
Lessons from the Life of David

BY SAM LAING

Scripture says he was "a man after God's own heart." What a tribute! From his days as a shepherd boy to his reign as Israel's king, David poured out his heart to God, demonstrated an amazing heart toward his best friend and to his worst enemy, struggled with sin that crept into his own heart, and wrote songs and psalms that still move our hearts three thousand years later. In this four-cassette series Sam Laing speaks with warmth, humor and deep conviction, showing today's disciples what they can learn from David's intensely personal walk with God. 4-cassette series.

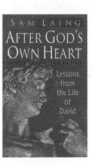

Generation Next

There is a spiritual battle raging for the minds and souls of preteens and teens. Parents must not be deceived; they must get in the fight for their children's faith. In the midst of all the world's influences, the greatest influence in a child's life is his or her parents and their spirituality.

These messages contain practical solutions and answers that make winning the battle possible. The call is for parents to run to the fight armed with the weapons of God. 4-cassette series.

Born Free

BY RYAN HOWARD

Three life-changing messages that will radically transform how you view who you are in Christ, how you can have confidence in your walk with God, and how to enjoy your life as a child of God. 3-cassette series.

*Biblically rich,
practically helpful
and just plain fun!*

**Dating
in the
Kingdom**

Jim and Teresa Brown

Dating in the Kingdom

BY JIM AND TERESA BROWN

Two leaders in the New York City church who married after many years as successful, fruitful singles in the Kingdom present material on Christian dating that is Biblically rich, practically helpful and just plain fun! Not just for steady dating couples, this series contains a broad range of material covering the whole gamut of dating in the kingdom. 3-cassette series.

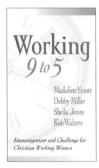

**Working
9 to 5**

Madaline Evans
Debby Miller
Sheila Jones
Kim Walters

*Encouragement and Challenge for
Christian Working Women*

Working 9 to 5
Encouragement and Challenge for Christian Working Women

Do you work 9 to 5 and sometimes feel "barely alive"? Do you want to be "spiritually alive" and to make an impact on the people around you? Can it be done? Four dynamic Christian working women say, "Absolutely, it can be!" This set offers the gift of Christian camaraderie to 9-to-5ers throughout the world. A great gift for a working woman and certainly a welcomed companion on your daily commute. 3-cassette series.

TAPE SERIES

DISCIPLING

GOD'S PLAN
TO TRAIN
AND TRANSFORM
HIS PEOPLE

Gordon Ferguson

Discipling

BY GORDON FERGUSON

Presenting material from the book by the same title on four cassettes. Dynamic lessons that will renew your passion for discipling relationships. Gordon teaches how God works through discipleship by sharing refreshingly personal accounts of discipling at work. He covers almost all facets of discipling, including authority and confidentiality.

To order call toll free in the US: 1-888-DPI-BOOK

For more information about ordering these and many other resources from DPI, call 1-888-DPI-BOOK or from outside the US: 781-937-3883 ext. 660.
worldwide web www.dpibooks.com